Unmanageable

UN MAN AGE ABLE

Leadership Lessons from an Impossible Year

JOHNATHAN NIGHTINGALE · MELISSA NIGHTINGALE

rawsignalpress

Published by Raw Signal Press
www.rawsignal.ca
We build better bosses.
For corporate/event bulk orders, contact press@rawsignal.ca

21 22 23 24 25 5 4 3 2 1

Deposit, Library and Archives Canada, 2021
ISBN-13: 978-0-9959643-2-7 (paperback)
ISBN-13: 978-0-9959643-3-4 (ebook)

To C, L, J, S, and B, all of whom
made cameos on work calls this past year.

May you enjoy in-person schooling
for years to come.

Contents

Introduction

We already know what they'll say.

When people write books about the impact of the COVID-19 pandemic on business, they'll talk about it as an accelerant. They'll talk about how it was a year that pulled the future forward. Remote work and remote conferences and remote weddings. Massive changes to consumer habits and the retail landscape. Lasting impacts to housing, travel, and tourism. They'll talk about how disruptive it was.

And somewhere, in the fourth paragraph of page 46, they'll acknowledge that it was a hard year. Maybe they'll use a word like *turmoil*, or *stressful*, or *burnout*.

This is a book about that word on page 46.

There is no way to talk about what happens next without standing in what the past year has been. But that won't stop folks from trying. Many of the business books about COVID-19 will be retrospectives, narratives constructed after the fact to help us make sense of a time that made no sense at all.

This is a book about what it felt like to live through it. Not a neatly packaged set of observations, gleaned from the benefit of hindsight. It's a snapshot. Of what it felt like to lead. And manage.

And parent. And live. Set against a backdrop of ever-changing public health guidelines and complicated trips to the grocery store.

We had already been writing our newsletter for years when the pandemic hit. Every other Wednesday we try to put something helpful into the world for bosses—something that makes you reflect and, if we really nail it, get more intentional about the way you lead.

Bosses are not the most lovable group of people from the outside. We are often underskilled, and when we make mistakes, the impact on our teams can be really painful. But underskilled isn't a permanent state. And that's the core of our work.

People aren't born knowing how to manage and lead a group in a work context. And if they aren't born knowing it, that means it's learnable. If you want to know why we sound optimistic, even on the heels of what the past year has been, that's why.

In our experience, most bosses want to be better. The vast majority want to do right by their people but struggle to figure out how—and find little support along the way.

This book is a year of love letters written to bosses throughout a global pandemic: 27 letters, from the first lockdowns to the first anniversary of those lockdowns.

At the close of the book, we talk about the mass renegotiation that is underway right now. How people are rethinking their relationship to work, and how organizations are racing to catch up. That renegotiation also has us feeling optimistic.

Wherever this finds you, we hope we're collectively in a better spot. A better spot around the virus, of course, but also around work and life and balance and boundaries. And, most importantly, around how bosses show up for their people.

· 1 ·

Our Job Now Is To Flatten the Curve

MARCH
11
2020

We're breaking our format this week. It wouldn't help to tell you what Melissa's reading and what Johnathan's reading. We're all reading the same thing. The COVID-19 coverage feels like it's everywhere, and it's overwhelming. If it feels that way for us, it probably feels that way for many of you, and for the people in your organizations. It's a lot. And as bosses, we have to do some really important work, starting right now.

First, a bit about where we are. Neither of us is a doctor (or an epidemiologist!), but the American Hospital Association is just crawling with those types of folk. When they had an expert on a few weeks ago to give a "best guess epidemiology" for the U.S. in the next little while, they got this:[1]

96,000,000 infections
4,800,000 hospitalizations
1,900,000 ICU admissions
480,000 deaths

What is hard to grasp, though, even from Big Scary Numbers like that, is what it means in lived experience. Yesterday a doctor from Bergamo, Italy, wrote about how things have changed for his city over the last week. It's harrowing. And it leaves no ambiguity about the lived experience.[2]

Scary things that we can't control are the worst scary things. The anxiety they cause can feed on itself. And it's always fair to ask ourselves if we're getting too worked up about it. We don't have answers for you there. We're onside with Jürgen Klopp when he says we should listen to the smart minds close to the problem.[3] But when we look around at the smartest minds in the room, closest to the problem, they sure do seem unanimous. Some bad stuff is coming.

And so we've been thinking a lot about flattening the curve.[4]

Since *The Economist* published the phrase "flatten the curve" three weeks ago, it's been the best advice we've found for bosses who ask us what they should be doing. We can't cure the virus (we're not doctors! or microbiologists!), but we can control how quickly it spreads. That matters, because every system has a breaking point, and we should want our health care systems to stay on the happy side of it. As bosses, there isn't much we can do to shrink the curve. But there is a lot we can do to flatten it.

Some of this is easy, like making sure your office has soap and sanitizer available. Suspending family-style lunches is probably smart, too. We recommend cancelling the apple-bobbing contest altogether. Anything you can do to minimize obvious opportunities for spread will flatten the curve.

Some of this is harder. Telling people to work from home when they're sick is great, but please think carefully about what support they need. Some of your people may feel like they *ought* to stay home, but if they're hourly and that means lost wages, you put them in a difficult situation. If leadership tells them to work from home but their own boss penalizes them for it or pressures them to stay, you're not going to succeed in flattening the curve.

There are people doing this right. Microsoft does not have a great history of treating their employees well, particularly women, but their leadership on this point is worth following.[5] Klick Health has made their phased coronavirus response guide public,[6] and it's a good template if you need one. The later phases of their guide include some scary questions. What happens if schools close? What happens when an employee is infected? However unwelcome those thoughts are, we would so much rather you think about them now than wait to react in the moment when they happen.

Some curve flattening is going to be pretty painful. We run events. And you may have noticed that event people are having a hard time. In the days leading up to Betterboss, we were keeping very close tabs on public health recommendations. We wanted to know whether we would have to cancel. We didn't, thankfully, but had we been a month further into this, we think we might have. That kind of cancellation would hit us hard. And every day we're seeing another SXSW, GDC, or Mobile World Congress announce a cancellation that hits their communities just as hard or harder.

As bosses, you're going to get a lot of questions from your people. Resist the urge to pretend it will all be fine. Even if you believe that, they don't. Resist the urge to play therapist, too. Now's not a time for bluffing—it's a time for getting the right supports in place.

We talk with bosses a lot about what a privilege it is to do this work. Sometimes they look at us funny. Amidst the vacation approvals and work assignments and promotion battles, it doesn't feel that way to them. But in moments like this, you have budget. You have influence over workload. You are invited to the management meetings. You have the ability to exercise discretion. You have privilege and sway and impact that your people don't. It's time to use it.

· 2 ·

What Do I Tell My Team?

MARCH
25
2020

"We just laid off half the company. And I want to say that will be the end of it. But I..."

"We have runway. Well, at least we *had* runway. But that was only as long as we had customers. And we did until..."

"My team keeps calling me. For meetings, but also for random stuff. Just to get on the phone. They need me to lead. But I don't know where we're going. Hell, I don't even know the situation for my own family. What am I supposed to tell them?"

. . .

We've been talking to bosses again. It's our thing that we do. And before all of this, it was our thing that we did all day every day. And we loved every fucking minute of it. How strange these last few weeks have felt—logging on after the kids have gone to bed, talking to Brady Bunch heads of bosses, spread out across time zones.

All wondering, "What do I tell my team?" And tucked in it, another question: "What should someone be telling me? 'Cause no one is, and I'm not comfortable winging something this big. I am way out of my depth."

First, don't bluff.

We start there. It's a thing we actually tell bosses all the time, not just during crises. But the rest of the time they nod. Like, of course I won't bluff. Who would? Why would they? But they all do. And the reason is simple.

As a boss you bluff when you think you ought to know. You bluff because your people are asking you for an answer. And if you don't have the answer, what does that say about your ability to lead? You felt like an imposter when they handed you the new business card in the first place. And isn't there that whole thing about everyone just making it up as they go along anyway?

We say don't *bluff*, because when you bluff people get hurt. The biggest fuck-ups are the ones where a leader's bluff gets called. And it will get called. We said it on last week's call with the bosses. People *want* certainty. And you can't give them that and they sort of already know it. But the thing they *absolutely cannot handle right now* is fuckery.

So don't bluff. That means saying what you know and being honest about the parts you don't. You may not know if people's jobs are safe, not even when there's a lot of pressure to tell them they'll be fine.

Second, figure out what you do know.

The stuff you knew last month might not be real anymore. What is our real runway now? What is our real business model now?[1] Sometimes figuring things out means asking very uncomfortable questions. Your own bosses may not have figured those things out yet, either.

The truth is that a lot of companies, maybe including yours, are not going to be able to make it through this level of global shutdown. And those that do are still facing down some scary math. So everything is already on the table. The question is whether the people in charge are seeing that clearly or being dragged to it, kicking and screaming. Your team isn't invited to some of the meetings that you are. And your voice carries more weight in some conversations. Ask until you hit something you believe.

Third, take care of you.

Back when we flew on airplanes, the line was "Always apply your own mask before assisting someone else." But as leaders, you are the glue. You are the connective tissue in your organization. And the level of coordination needed to go from in-office to fully remote/distributed means your calendar is positively fuuuuucked. So we get that you might be having trouble with masks right now.

So many leaders are coming into this pandemic on the heels of years of manufactured crises. They were tired before they reached the starting line for this particular race. And now their tanks are empty.

You are no good to nobody running on empty.

You need rest. You need food. We know you feel like you need to be there for your team no matter the hour, no matter how many of these unscheduled calls you've already taken. But this will take resilience. Breathe fresh air before you log on. Try to sign off before it gets dark. Figure out what helps you to refill the tank. And do those things. There's a long road ahead.

Fourth, lead.

We know, it's an impossible ask. G-d. Lead? To where? And for what? We get it. No one can see the future right now, and it feels like from that place we're all guessing.

So okay. So we finally gave in this weekend and sat down with our kids to watch *Frozen 2*. After a week of homeschooling while doomscrolling,[2] we let the weekend take more than its fair share of screens.

Anyway, there's this scene pretty early on (no spoilers!) where the elder troll is talking to Anna and Elsa about the future. And he can't see it. He's a pretty magical fella, but he can't get this one clear. And he says, "When one can see no future, all one can do is the Next Right Thing."

Can you believe that line is just sitting there in that movie, waiting for you?

Take care of yourselves. Take care of your teams. Don't try to get ahead of a global pandemic—that's not a thing that's helpful to reach for right now. Just find the next right thing for your people. And then do that. And then wake up and do it again tomorrow.

· 3 ·

Top 10%, Bottom 10%

APRIL
8
2020

We don't claim this as our format—we learned it from our own advisers—but it's a good one. It goes like this: There are plenty of other places for your middle 80%. What we want in this room are the things that are going so well that we should celebrate and the things that are so wretched that you need help to get through them.

It's masterful as a facilitation tool. But it's also handy at clearing out the filler so we can get to the real stuff.

These past few weeks, we've been talking to bosses about their top 10% and bottom 10%. And in the last few days, something important has shifted.

We heard from bosses who felt very in their top 10%. Where things had shifted in good ways, and they felt some solid earth under their feet for the first time in weeks.

And we had others very in their bottom 10%. People who have been running *so hot* trying to keep everything going for the last few weeks. And it isn't enough. And their batteries are empty. And they need help.

Wherever you see yourself in that, *remember that the people you work with might be somewhere very different.* And so, a couple of thoughts.

If you are finding your way out of the fog, your job is to bring other people with you. If you've found a routine that works. If you're running again. If you're sleeping again. If you're cooking more and ordering in less. We need you. There are a lot of us still in the fog, and it's not a thing we can wish away. But if you are up above it, you can see farther than we can, and *clarity is incredible valuable right now.*

So write it down. Be present in email and Slack and wherever the rest of us are. Speak up on calls that sound foggier than you feel, particularly if you can see which work is important and which work isn't these days—we need to know, so we can stop working on the wrong stuff we haven't realized is wrong stuff.

Don't impose it on us. From a foggy place, someone else being too shiny can be irritating. But offer it. Especially to the folks on your team. Do not, do not, *do not* assume that it must be obvious to them, too. In fog, nothing is obvious. Be generous with your clarity.

If, on the other hand, you are still in the fog, *slow down.* It's not safe to move fast in a fog. The good news is that some people are starting to get some clarity, and help might be on the way soon. But in the meantime, stop trying to see through it by just burning hotter and hotter. Every driver's-ed class knows this. High beams don't work in fog—you just get glare that makes it even harder to see.

If you're a boss in fog, we need you to invest in your own resilience first. From a depleted place, you're no good to your team. It feels heroic to sacrifice yourself to lighten the load for others, and to a point that's a job we're paid to do as bosses. But if you've gotten to an unhealthy place, please pull in supports and take a rest.

If your company is betting on burnout as a strategy, that's no kind of plan. Things are different. Organizations do need to move fast. Things are different. Organizations do need to move fast and the stakes are high. But if your company is trying to juggle multiple crises right now, we have bad news. All they're saying is that they haven't decided which crisis is the most important. Because realistically, it's impossible to address all of them at once. The only choice you have is whether to wreck yourself and your team on the way to realizing that. Hospitals are one of the only organizations expressly built to handle multiple crises at once and, tragically, we're all learning that they have limits, too.

Sleep. Eat well. Exercise. Take quiet time. Get therapy. If you're in fog and can't seem to get out, please start there. Not with the emails. Or Slack pings. Or the Zoom call that's impossibly scheduled against your quarantine-altered home life.

This week seemed to be a turning point for a lot of bosses. But we are not done with this thing. There will be optimistic top-10% moments and crushing bottom-10% ones in the weeks to come. We've all got a long way to go yet. Take care of yourself. And each other.

· 4 ·

The End of the Beginning

APRIL
22
2020

So, there's this thread from Arthur Chu where he talks about research done on survival—survivors of plane crashes, shipwrecks, mountain climbs gone bad, whatever.[1] We've read some of those books, too. The thread is glib in parts and comes from a "tough love" place that you may not have the energy for right now. But the core of it is a thing we believe:

> Your ability, your team's ability, your organization's ability to survive a crisis like this starts when you accept it for what it is.

This is an unpleasant thing to believe, because COVID-19 is a shitty and unfair and unearned thing, and it's fucking up a bunch of stuff. Stuff that you cared about and still want to see happen.

So you might not be there yet, and that's okay. That grief article we all read last month didn't put a time limit on things.[2] You have to *feel all the feelings* to get to acceptance. You can't skip steps.

But the sense we have is that more of us *are* getting to that acceptance point now. We've been in mourning for a month or more, and we've gotten to the sad-calm place. The *enduring it* place. And, like…

NOW WHAT?

We were talking with a close friend the other day and she said,

> "Everything I'm reading is that I have to throw away all my old plans. And okay. I get it. But I liked my old plans. 😟"

The 😟 was audible.

The business/strategy thinkers are all yelling (they're always yelling) at you that you must throw away everything you've ever known. That nothing will ever be the same. That all your plans are gone, and every assumption must be questioned. *Who knows, in a post-COVID-19 world, if we'll even still have offices, or cars, or Tuesdays??*

Even from a place of acceptance it's all just...a lot.

We took the title of this week's letter from Alex Danco's most recent post.[3] He makes a bunch of his own predictions that you can take or leave. But he says one thing that is very true: We're at the end of the beginning. We know roughly which cards each country and industry and family has been dealt. We're nowhere close to done, but we're done with getting started.

And the next part is going to feel very slow by comparison.

WHAT HAPPENS NEXT

A lot of us are very bad at slow. Nothing about modern life gives us room to practice. We listen to podcasts while commuting while scrolling through our newsfeeds and responding to emails using predictive text to make it all go faster.

We suck at this.

In our rush to make it all go faster, we've ported the trappings of urgency into our homes—what used to be our quiet place to close the door on the rush and freneticism, to Netflix and also to chill. The place that represented solace and safety for so many of us is now just an unending ride on a crowded city bus. We are trying to juggle work and family and friends and feeding ourselves and sterilizing everything.

We are staying the fuck home but we have yet to sit the fuck down.

The first wave of acceptance is bidding adieu to our old way of life. The next wave starts by slowing down. If you're bored out of your gourd already and that sounds terrifying, hear me out.

The things rushing in to fill your boredom right now aren't helping.

The unending parade of prediction pieces about a post-COVID-19 world are noise. And fear. And capitalist pron. They paint a fantasy about how quickly we can get back to full productivity and high-water marks of consumer spending habits.

We need all of our effort and energy focused on how we *get to* the post-COVID-19 world, not on hypothesizing on whether children will still have birthday parties and whether they will still eat cake. Those aren't the interesting questions. And if history is any indication, we're woefully bad at guessing at this stuff anyway.

Acceptance means we stop living in a prediction and start living in the now.

The yogis say Be Here Now.

That's the challenge for all of us as we head into this next phase—out of the hectic, new-information-every-day, everything-swirling-chaos phase and into the middle part. The I'm-bored, my-family-is-bored, every-day-is-Groundhog-Day, and I-am-all-out-of-ways-to-make-chickpeas-interesting phase–

People say, "Get comfortable with being uncomfortable." And they say it like it's a choice. There's a reason we resist being uncomfortable. First, it's, well, *uncomfortable*. And given a choice between that and comfort, it's not surprising many people opt for the latter.

But the people who say it want us to know that the discomfort is where a lot of the growth happens. And if we run from it, we're missing out on a lot of the deep internal work, the transformative stuff that has us grappling with hard questions—questions about who we are, what we care about, who we care about, what we want to do with our time on Earth, and what we'd trade to be truly happy and content. Modern life doesn't make time for these questions because so much of modern life relies on us not looking too closely.

We're all home. Billions of us, around the globe, are sitting at home. Here's the thing to remember about the next phase: **It's *your* home. You get to choose what you invite in. Now is the time to quiet the noise and reclaim your space.** Even if it's just in bits and pieces after the kids go to sleep.

When all this is over, what will you want to have done with that space?

· 5 ·

This Is Nothing Like Mat Leave

MAY
6
2020

When we were first at home, we joked that it felt like a collective parental leave. With human, pet, and plant babies. Of various ages. Around the entire globe.

There are familiar elements. The boredom. The oppressive, unending boredom. The complex relationship with leaving the house, where even a small trip to the grocery store is a massive endeavor. The urgent need to fix things that your eyes bounced off of for years. The desire to burn your stretchy pants so you can start over with something stylish and chic when you next encounter the world.

But on parental leave, you can still meet up with friends. You find other people going through the same experience and go for coffee. And your starting point is usually something lovely and joyful.

This doesn't feel like that. In some important ways, this feels more like divorce.

YOU WERE BOTH MARRIED BEFORE, RIGHT?

Yup. We were early adopters of divorce. Getting divorced in your early thirties means you are the reference point and sounding board for everyone else as they wonder whether it's time. We don't mind. Divorce Club is a good club—albeit with some painful initiation fees.

Divorce is this thing where everything you thought you knew is suddenly upside down. It is a prolonged phase of having the rug pulled out from under you. And again. And then again. Until you think you've found your footing—only to find that that wasn't new footing after all. New footing would still be many, many rug pulls away. There is no joy in divorce. Even when there is relief, or moments of forgetting how awful everything has been, there isn't really joy.

And there's this step in the process that is particularly awful. Even when you warn people, almost no one manages to avoid it. It's the *one last chance.* The *maybe we can still make this work.* The *remember how good it was.* Holly Brockwell wrote about her own lockdown-amplified version.[1] And around the world thousands of us quietly poured a glass of wine for her.

It never goes well.

It's so hard to skip, because the remembering is powerful. That last gasp of who you were is so loud. So appealing. You need to know if you can still go back or not. And the recoil is so sudden.

Because what you realize in that moment is that divorce is also a process of transformation. The tearing down is also a rebuilding. And you aren't the person from those memories anymore. Those memories might be great—they can still be great memories—they just aren't who you are today.

HOW DOES GOING BACK TO WORK FEEL?

Eight weeks ago things here in Toronto started to shut down. And if they'd only shut down for a week or two, maybe we all could have gone back to what it was. But it's been two months. You're different than you were. We all are.

We're hearing from more and more people that they don't want to go back to the old thing. It's not who they are anymore. They're putting off the conversation with their bosses until things stabilize, but it's coming. The decision's already made. The old thing isn't a fit anymore. Even the VCs are saying, "Like it or not, there is about to be a huge reshuffling of talent."[2]

For some it's the role itself. But for many more, it's the things around the work. It's the commute that added multiple hours to an already full day. Or the realization that what once passed for work–life balance never was and surely isn't anymore. How could it be? Once you know the thing, you can't unknow.

And others of you are still hoping to go back and make it work. Many of you will, to be clear. This isn't musical chairs; you're not required to change seats. But some of you have a nagging feeling that gets louder anytime someone talks about going back to the office. You might still have to give it one last chance to know for sure. It won't take long for you to figure it out.

So here's the deal. If you already know you need a change, or if you're very certain you're still in the right place, great. Clarity is a special thing these days, and we're glad you have it.

If you're a boss wondering what kind of team you're going to get back, be open to what's coming. It will be different from the team you had two months ago. Some of your team will be happy to be back. Some will need to start fundamental conversations about their role and their future. The brilliant leaders in the year to come will be the ones who can meet their people where they are.

And if you're someone on the bubble—if you have been nodding along to all the talk about transformation and divorce and we've put a name on something you've been feeling and you're wondering what the answer is for *you*—well...

The hardest part about divorce is high bridges. It's standing at the top knowing you have to get off, and looking over the edge. Not because you want to hurt yourself, but because the only way off this path is into the unknown, without being sure if anyone or anything will catch you. It's the moment when you have to trust that eventually it'll all come together again. And while that will look totally different, there's the hope that the new thing may be even more wonderful than you can imagine. But first you gotta jump. And that shit is terrifying.

The first rule of Divorce Club is *The moment before the jump is worse than the fall.*

· 6 ·

But How Do I Know They're Working?

MAY
20
2020

We were part of the first wave of internet-enabled, globally distributed work. The first time we managed, we weren't in the same office as the people on our teams. Often we weren't even in the same country. And when we talked about working with folks all over the globe, one question came up more than any other. At the time it always seemed silly.

But how do you know they're working? If you aren't in the same place and those people are working at home, how do you know they're actually working?

Our response was always the same: If they're sitting at a desk in your office, how do you know they're working? How do you know they aren't just daydreaming or researching their next vacation?

There's a lot of bosses trying to figure this one out right now. Their people aren't where they can see them. So they ask the very silly, surface-level, unexamined, first-time-working-with-remote-folks question. How do I know they're working?

And the answer some bosses have come up with is to fix the "I can't see them" part. To solve their own management discomfort at the expense of their employee's privacy.

Employee surveillance isn't a new idea, but it's finding new fans.[1] There is software out there that bosses can buy that will track your activity. Which apps you have open. Which websites you visit. How long you take to go to the bathroom.

A reporter at the *New York Times* tried it out with his own boss a few weeks ago. The results were so creepy that his boss bailed out of the experiment.[2] How nice it must be, to be able to opt out. To have the power in the organization to treat this kind of thing as a curiosity you're tired of. Most people don't get that chance. For many people, this is just the latest little indignity they have to endure to keep their job.

It doesn't even work, of course. Management by surveillance rarely does. And you already know why. When you track bathroom breaks, you have employees bring their laptops to the bathroom. Does that sound healthy? When you track mouse movement, you get employees who are super adept at keeping a mouse moving, or who have figured out that an oscillating fan and a pair of chopsticks can do it for them. Is that the business you're in? Mouse moving? If not, we suggest measuring something that actually matters.

The truth is that it's a trap to even approach this kind of tool on its merits. To argue over whether it's effective is to accept the premise that if it *were* effective, it would be a good idea. It isn't.

THE THIRD CATEGORY

We've had a thing stuck in our craw for a few weeks now. Can two people have a shared craw? A common set of hackles? Anyway it came from the loveliest of all places, which is (obviously) Anne Helen Peterson's newsletter.

In the middle of an otherwise on-target essay,[3] she writes:

> And I get it: these massive, massively profitable companies are trying to survive. They are simply following the logic of capitalism, which demands that profit trump consideration for human life. All companies that treat its workers like humans do so either because they're forced to (by unions and labor laws and regulations) or because of leadership that's figured out that treating workers like humans actually makes them more productive and profitable.

Do you see the trap again? The effectiveness framing? This idea that treating your workers well happens either because you're forced to or because you realized it was profitable.

Yes, it's more profitable to treat your people well. There are whole books on this subject.[4] And yes, unions and labor protections are vitally important. But so is having a spine and some fucking decency.

There's a third category of boss here: leaders who treat their employees well *because their employees are human beings.* Because no business exists except for the labor of its people. Fuck the effectiveness argument. There needs to be dignity in work regardless. And as leaders, it's on us to ensure that we protect that.

We know there's a third category because we meet them every day. Bosses who are uncomfortable with the power they have but are trying to be responsible with it. Bosses who recognize that their impact is not something they can pretend away or delegate to an app.

The week we launched Managing 2020, we had bosses

ordering it on their personal credit cards. For themselves. And for the managers on their teams. Because they needed help supporting their people but didn't want to ask their company to fund it in the middle of a fucking pandemic so they just did it 'cause it needed doing. Not gonna lie, when we figured out what was happening, we had a little cry here at RSG WFH HQ. 😢

There is a third category of bosses, and we need a LOT more of them. We need leaders who recognize the trappings of power without abdicating it. We need bosses who show up with empathy and kindness, and who don't see that as somehow at odds with profitability or getting shit done. It's not. Our whole gig is about growing the third category. But we need help. We're not getting there nearly fast enough. And the result is that the two-types-of-shitty-bosses conundrum persists.

Red Rover–style, we need to find people from the cynical bossing groups and call them over. And we need to lift up skilled new leaders who will straight up outperform their lazy, surveillance-dependent peers. We can't let those fuckers off the hook. It's very, very hard to prevent power from accumulating in organizations. But we can and should expect that the people wielding that power to do so with empathy, and kindness.

Treat your people well. Invest in *them* instead of tools to spy on them. Not just because it is more profitable, but because it's the right fucking thing to do.

· 7 ·

Is Anyone Really Thinking about Work Right Now?

JUNE
3
2020

[On May 25, the killing of George Floyd by Minneapolis police officers set off a summer of worldwide protests against police brutality and racism. By the time this newsletter came out, a week later, the protests had reached such an intensity that hundreds of U.S. cities had imposed curfews and more than half the states in the U.S. had activated the national guard.]

It's early.

We're writing Tuesday morning for you to read Wednesday. We're reading the news from last night, and wondering how much will change in the next 24 hours. It's safe to say that neither of us got a full night's sleep. Maybe you didn't, either.

We're thinking about the last week. Upheaval and suffering in a year already overfull of upheaval and suffering. And, to be honest, we're wondering if there's anything to say to bosses right now. Is anyone really thinking about work? Is it even our place to speak, today?

It's a worthwhile question to ask. As white/white-passing people, we're always in danger of shoving ourselves into conversations we don't have a place in. We learn early that we get to occupy every space. And it's work to unlearn that, so it's a worthwhile question to ask. But it also has an answer: We don't get to sit this one out. As Keosha Love says, we've got to pull the fuck up.

PULL THE FUCK UP

Our Black readers don't need us to tell them anything about how to fight the oppression they face. That's not our lane.

But we're hearing from non-Black bosses that they don't know what they should do. They know there are a lot of things not to do. And some of them feel tempted to just sit quietly until this passes, for fear of getting it wrong. But they know it and you know it, too: That's not solidarity. So let's talk about pulling the fuck up.

AS A HUMAN BEING

Pulling the fuck up has two dimensions in this newsletter: as human beings and as bosses. These are closely related. First, as a human:

- **Read this:** "Welcome to the Anti-Racism Movement—Here's What You've Missed."[1] Watching Ijeoma Oluo write is breathtaking. She is surgical and vulnerable and honest and clear. She wrote this back in 2017, but it holds up. If the outrage of the last few weeks has you referring to protesters and activists as "we" instead of "they," it's time to read this. It will not be comfortable. Surgery isn't.
- **Then act.** March if you can, but don't fuck shit up. Our job in a march like this is solidarity and protection, not spray-painting a Starbucks.

- **Act.** Come get your people—your family, friends, and colleagues who don't get it. Don't ignore it when they talk about "Black-on-Black violence" or say, "If they were peaceful, the police wouldn't shoot them with rubber bullets and tear gas." Make things uncomfortable. Be less polite.
- **Act.** Support organizations that are close to this problem and have been working it for a long time. COVID has made things hard on a lot of folks, we know. But there are a lot of ways to help,[2] and there is power in numbers. Just don't get dazzled and put it off—this is a thing to do now.

AS A BOSS

Back at the beginning of the pandemic we wrote this:

> We talk with bosses a lot about what a privilege it is to do this work. Sometimes they look at us funny. Amidst the vacation approvals and work assignments and promotion battles, it doesn't feel that way to them. But in moments like this, you have budget. You have influence over workload. You are invited to the management meetings. You have the ability to exercise discretion. You have privilege and sway and impact that your people don't. It's time to use it.

That's still true. So, as a boss,

- **Read this:** "Hey Employers: Do Black Lives Matter?"[3] Pariss Athena did the free work for us all of collecting a thread of ideas for how employers can support their Black employees, as offered by Black employees. Not by other folks imagining what might help.

- **Then act.** Pariss lays it out. Talk about what's going on (without offering your own unhelpful takes). Give your Black employees space and permission to be low productivity. Better yet, proactively offer them time off if they want it. Don't make them do all the work to lay out your allyship for you. Don't demand ally points or "one of the good ones" credit for doing this. And listen without defensiveness if they tell you that something you're doing isn't what they need.
- **Act.** Most businesses have corporate-giving budgets, employee-matching programs. Do you know what yours are? If they don't exist, now's a good time to push for them. We know that COVID-19 has tightened everyone's budgets. It's certainly tightened ours. But fuck it, what's the point of running a business if you can't use it to make things better? If it helps to have a place to start, we're sending money to BLM Toronto, Raheem, National Bail Fund Network, and Justice for Regis.
- **Act.** It's not enough to give out of one budget while propping up racism elsewhere. As a boss, you get to shove your company toward antiracism beyond the charitable-giving policy. Are your products helping awful people be awful? Is your company holding a "neutral" stance that, in practice, means you're supporting the groups that fuel hate?[4] Time to make things uncomfortable there, too.

We know. It's a lot. A thing we appreciate so much about all of you is that you don't need us to just be fluffy and light about this work. That you let us talk about heavy shit when we need to. We're in a heavy spot right now, and we all have work to do. Thank you for doing the work. It's worth doing. Black lives matter.

(If the work is wearing you down. Or if just... all of this is wearing you down, please remember that there are resources out there for you.[5] There is no shame in mental health struggle. Not now. Not ever.)

· 8 ·

Are We Gonna Talk about That Asterisk?

JUNE
17
2020

We talk with people about work. That's our life. Sometimes with founders, executive directors, and CEOs. Sometimes with mid-career leaders, or new managers coming up. And sometimes with folks who are early in their careers and trying to figure it all out for the first time.

A surprising thing is that a lot of those conversations sound the same. Regardless of seniority, almost everyone wonders if they're making the right calls for their career. Almost everyone wants to know how they can build better balance in their work life. Almost everyone worries that they don't know what they don't know.

But on certain topics, at certain times, the conversations diverge. The CEOs say one thing, and their investors, and executives, and cofounders agree. But the rest of the staff say something very different.

We are in one of those divergent times.

Here's roughly how it goes. We ask the CEOs, the founders, the exec directors how things are going and they say, "Great. We pivoted the whole business to remote and online within the first week of lockdowns. There's been no dip in productivity, and frankly, we're not sure we're ever going back to the way things were before."

The first time we heard it, we assumed it was ego. Who are these people who feel like the adjustments to their business that happened in mid-March were a *mild refactoring*? Well, it turns out there are a LOT of them. You can't swing a stick right now without hitting a CEO thought-leadering about the end of offices.

So then we talk to the non-founder, non-C-suite bosses and employees. *How are you?* we ask. *How are things going?* And what comes back is this.

I'm good.*

I'm fine.*

We're doing okay.*

We're all healthy.*

You see it? That asterisk*? You can hear it in their voices. You might be able to hear it in your own. As more of us are joining town hall meetings from in front of our shower curtains, the asterisk is a way to reclaim some space between us and our work. And you know that if you pick at that scab: you'd better be braced. Because honestly, any number of things can happen next.

FUEL LIGHT

When we talk to bosses about performance plans, we warn them about the boom/bust pattern. We tell that that often, putting an employee on a performance plan generates a rush of output, a huge lift in productivity. And as a boss it feels so good to imagine that things are turning around. There's such a hopefulness to it. But what you can't see is that the employee suddenly putting up big numbers is doing things they can't sustain. They are burning themselves red hot to reach your notion of "acceptable." And at some point they run out of fuel.

That asterisk is a fuel light. That's people running out of gas. It's being so worn that you're just smiling politely and hoping no one asks a follow-up question. Because you do *not* have the energy for a follow-up question.

To the CEOs and founders who are merrily assuming the complete overhaul of the modern workforce went by unremarked by their staff? Careful. You can fall so in love with the story you're telling and the route you're driving that you miss the fuel light.

One possibility is that your story is true, sure. But another possibility is that your people are broken and tired and depleted—so much so that they lack the words to even articulate it, or the time to fully grok their relative level of exhaustion. We ran a session with a group of leaders last week where we asked them how they were *actually* doing. Some of them said, "I haven't really let myself answer that for three months."

WHAT COMES NEXT

There's a bunch of research about belonging at work,[1] and the idea that how connected we feel to our colleagues and our own boss has a profound impact on how we show up in the role. We can all call up anecdotes in our own work when we felt that connection, or missed it. But it's nice to see those anecdotes mapped to the collective. It's not just you. It's *all* of us. Three months ago, our sense of belonging at work was disrupted on a global scale.

As we start to look toward what happens next, we're thinking a lot about the asterisk and about what it means that the people in charge think everything is fine while the people doing the work are breaking down at night and putting on a brave face for Zoom calls in the morning.

For the bosses telling us that everything's great, the answer is pretty easy. They're in for some surprises. Expect siloing and conflict and misunderstandings. Expect a lot of delayed-onset turnover. People who are burning out might still need this job, but if your organization isn't creating a climate for them to recover, expect them to leave once they're able. That's when you'll see your productivity hit.

For the folks who haven't had space in the past couple of months to think past the asterisk: we get it. We don't pretend that it's easy to throw yourself fearlessly into self-examination—it makes us tired just writing it—but it's worth carving out some time. A natural response to crisis is to compartmentalize and constrict. To close ourselves up, even to ourselves. Maybe you still need to be in that place, to protect yourself and what little fuel you have left. That's okay.

We don't know what the next phase of work will feel like. But we do know that whatever comes next, it's on the other side of that asterisk. Rebuilding a global workforce's sense of belonging is gonna take time. But it starts with being able to genuinely answer the question "How are you?" At least for yourself.

. . .

* *Our amazing friend Saadia Muzaffar was the first person we heard put a name to the "asterisk" that people are using as invisible punctuation these days. We reference it here, with permission and gratitude.*

· 9 ·

You'd Know the Answer for Sidewalk Chalk

JULY
1
2020

Last week, we were on the hunt for sidewalk chalk. It's one of the few socially distant city-kid activities. After trying local stores and Amazon, we finally found two tiny boxes. Now the first thing the little kid does is grab a pack and head outside where a bunch of other kids are playing. Within moments, she's torn apart the entire pack and distributed them to a few kids on our street. They all begin to color and we're watching as the sticks turn to nubs.

This was on the heels of multiple days. Multiple failed trips to stores. Multiple internet searches. Mask. Sanitize. Ask. Sanitize. Try again. Navigate shitty, poorly rendered CSS. Put items in cart. Send an e-transfer 'cause they don't accept credit cards. Call to find out when to pick up the order. No one answers. Head to store. Mask. Sanitize. Ask. Sanitize. Bring chalk home.

Within ten minutes, the chalk is in pieces. The kids are having a great time.

Happy kids. Sharing. Playing nicely, yet distantly. But as we watch them, mixed in with the joy is something else—a feeling of scarcity, like there's not enough. The multi-day loop to get four pieces of chalk only to have them disappear instantaneously is one more thing we don't have time or energy for. Everything takes so long right now. Every trip to the store is a bingo card of potential violations. Did you touch the door on the way in? Did you remember to hit the crosswalk button with your elbow? Do these places even sanitize the top of the sanitizer bottles? 'Cause every person smashes their hand against it the moment they walk in the door.

It's exhausting. We're on day 100-something and we're all very tired. And from that tired place, we had a scarcity reaction to small children playing with toys. It's a pretty fucked-up reason to get grumpy. But maybe you can hand-wave at the whole tired parents thing and not think we're terrible humans. That's kind of you. Thank you for that.

GROWN-UP SCARCITY

Last week, we were on a call with a bunch of founders and CEOs, and when we opened for Q&A, someone asked if the pandemic meant companies could offer lower salaries. Basic supply-and-demand principles. A lot of people got laid off and are in a precarious situation. They might not have many job offers lined up. Many orgs are freezing hiring. Can a company with open roles pay less to new hires who join during a recession?

And lest you think it was one dude being shady on the CEO call, we promise it was not. We had someone reach out after receiving a job offer that was a 15% reduction in base comp and a demotion in title. And the employer had shrugged and said, "Yeahbutpandemic, amirite?"

Landlords exploiting people.[1] Employers playing games with compensation. Neighbors hoarding sidewalk chalk. That thing with the toilet paper. The preppers were largely wrong about our immediate response to crisis, but they were right that in persistent crisis, many of us would find it hard to be our best selves. Our instincts are moving from collective to individual. And even when the results are disastrous, a lot of folks are very tired of having to think about others.

Okay so great. So we're all wrung out. We're all feeling our assholish tendencies rising to the surface. We're all getting grabby in the sandbox with literal four-year-olds. Now what? Well, there's an easy part and a hard part to that.

THE EASY PART IS KNOWING WHAT TO DO

You do. You know what to do with the salaries and with the sidewalk chalk: Start with community. Tech has co-opted *community* to mean "the people who post on my newsfeed." We *don't* mean them, or at least not only them. We mean the humans you share space with—your customers, neighbors, and friends; the families of your employees.

What is the choice you can make that feeds your community? Of the available options, even if they'll never hear about it, which is the one you'd be proud for your community to know about? Do that one.

Community is an ancient concept for humans—much more ancient than the concept of shareholder value. And even with all of a community's complexity and internal disagreements, it's pretty easy to guess how they would respond to decisions like these. The community wants you to treat your workers with dignity. The community wants you to share the sidewalk chalk. Communities play the long game, and communities remember who played a short one.

The easy part is knowing what to do.

THE HARD PART IS DOING IT

Much of the world is still in lockdown. And some of the places no longer locked down are seeing horrifying surges. We passed 500,000 dead over the weekend. And we're more than a month into daily global marches against anti-Black racism and police violence.

And like, where are you supposed to put all of that? If you're a leader of people right now—no, fuck that—if you're a human being right now, it's a lot to reckon with. The empathy-exhaustion and the anger that comes with just engaging with the state of the world these days? Those are real.

In the midst of all that, you can know what to do and still have a hard time doing it. You can know that a crisis calls on us all to support each other and still find yourself pulling away. You will want to keep that budget, and that sidewalk chalk, close to you and away from everyone else.

Sometimes you're going to give in to that want, is our prediction. And maybe you'll feel like shit for it afterward. We don't have a cool management tool with a funny acronym for that. We're in the long haul now, and we're nowhere near the end. You can rise to a crisis, try to be a rock for those around you, and still have days when you lose the fortitude to be your best self.

Instead, the thing we can offer you is this: Community is stronger than that. It's stronger than you having a rough patch. Community isn't one action; it's the sum of our actions. As long as you're in the seat—as a leader or as a human—you get to make the calls on how you show up. And that means that if you were a lesser, scarcer, grabbier self yesterday, well, you have a chance to be better today.

Listen, when we get through this—and we will get through this—each of our organizations will either be here or it won't. And maybe you worry that the cost of taking care of people means your company risks not being here. Well, that's a risk regardless. That's at risk even if you cut every corner and exploit every advantage over your employees. The question is, is it worth it to have a company that survives the pandemic at any cost? Are those choices you'd be proud of?

We're being asked as bosses to make choices between the well-being of the communities we live in and the company we help run. In almost every case, the idea that those things are in conflict is a lie. We should all refuse to play that game. But in the cases where they are in conflict, or where we're forced to pretend that they are, we have a choice to make. *You* have a choice to make. Companies don't have intrinsic value. People do.

Choose people.

· 10 ·

Checkmate in Five Moves

JULY
15
2020

Last week we had childcare. It was fleeting; we only got a week of it. But for the first time in 112 days, we had five hours a day of uninterrupted work. We went to the office and everything—just the two of us.

Parenting during COVID is this relentless paradox of loving the time and struggling to endure it. And so the COVID-polite thing to do when you hear that parents have gotten their first taste of childcare is to gush. *Oh my god, was it so amazing? Did you get giddy at being able to finish a coffee while it was still warm, or an article, or a thought?*

"Giddy" doesn't really describe it. You know when you close your eyes, take a deep breath in, and slowly breathe it out? And you feel your shoulders relax and your neck gets that warm tingle? It's much closer to relief than giddiness. And when you open your eyes again, sometimes you find you have some clarity you didn't have a minute ago.

40 PERCENT

At lunch, we would walk around in our masks. Raw Signal HQ is in a retail-heavy, tourist-focused part of Toronto, and we weren't sure what to expect. In March, in the last days before lockdown, it was a ghost town.

Now the businesses are all open. There are happy little distance circles all over the place, like a live-action Bil Keane comic.[1] Every store has their doors wide open, despite the unending heat, so you'll know that they're open. Staff members stand out front, smiling behind their masks, to make sure you know they're open. They need you to know they're open.

We talk to business owners—in the retail district where our office is based and also in the broader tech community—and right now they're all using the same number. *We're at about 40%*. The ones that have been open throughout and the ones that opened just a few weeks ago. *We're at about 40%. We'd be at 10%, but we got creative with this and that and so now we're at 40% of what we were pre-COVID.*

There aren't many businesses that can survive operating at 40% long-term. The open doors and smiling staff belie a thing that was clear to us everywhere we went last week: their rents are in arrears, and it's even worse than it appears.

People talk about COVID as an accelerant. That if your business was struggling before all this, you're likely in worse shape now.[2] That's true for business owners, but it's also true for everything else in your life. Jobs, roommates, friendships, marriages[3]—everything is under strain. All of it is somewhere along the COVID Richter scale, where things are shaken but we're not yet sure where they'll shake out.

Forty percent is a hard number because it's large enough to give you some hope but small enough that it can still feel hopeless. What really matters is the direction of it. Is it 40% on the way back up to 80%, or a 40% bounce on the way back down to zero? Are these aspects of your life on the way from depletion back to fullness? Or are they a falling knife?

It's hard to know, from the outside looking in, the direction of someone else's 40%. It can be hard to know from the inside, too. But sometimes you really do have a strong gut sense.

CHECKMATE IN FIVE MOVES

Chess players do this. If you watch tournaments, there's often a moment when one player will put their king down on the board and call it. They are out of moves. If you don't play chess, it can seem like poor form to give up before the end. But they can see how the next five moves have to go. And once you're out of moves, there's no point in playing out the rest of the game. No amount of divine intervention can change the pieces on the board. The losing player is eager to reset the pieces and start a new game.

We resist chess analogies most of the time because chess is a game where you have all the information, and life usually isn't. But sometimes it's exactly that clear. Sometimes you can see the board and you know how it will end and your only choice is what you do with that news.

Calling a mated board feels like failure because *it is.* You lost. The question in that moment isn't "Would you like to fail?" It's "Do you want to fail fast or slow? Can you acknowledge it yet, or do we have to play it all the way out?" Once it's clear that there isn't an unlimited number of moves on the board, there are only two choices: put it down or keep going.

We know the answer we're supposed to choose. Hell, startup culture is all about the celebration of fast failure. But outside of startup bravado, in actual real life, we don't always do it. We routinely pick slow failure. We stay in the job because we have some unsubstantiated hope that it will get better. We convince ourselves we're *still learning*, that there are moves on the board we've yet to explore. The decision is already made, but we're moving through life like we're still contemplating it.

So we come back to the question from earlier. Are you at 40% on your way back to 80? Or is it already clear to you that things are heading in the other direction?

AND THEN WHAT HAPPENS?

We don't want to be downers. Reality has enough of that right now. And if your 40% is rising, don't let us push you off that high. To be enduring 2020 and actually have a business, a relationship, a career that is rising up is a hell of a thing. For you, all we can say is "Good work," and we hope you'll take time to celebrate.

For those of you who see yourself in the 40%-and-falling camp, though, it's time to see it for what it is. If it's genuinely changeable and you have the energy and the commitment to change it, we're rooting for you. If it's not changeable, though, well...

More time is wasted in those last five moves, in that slow march from 40% down to zero. It's depressing to accept that a new move isn't going to appear. But it's also so freeing to put down the shit that isn't serving you anymore. To call it on the relationships that have been over for a long time. To flip over a board where you didn't have any moves and reset the pieces so you can start again.

That doesn't mean quit today. There is zero shame offered or expected for staying in a safe-but-not-great situation until the storms of 2020 pass. But if you already know how this game ends, you can at least start setting up the pieces for the next one.

· 11 ·

The Waiting Is the Hardest Part

JULY
29
2020

Remember a few months ago when we told you the waiting would be the hardest part?[1] We're here now.

Waiting for school to start. Or for school to not start. Waiting to get back to the office. Or for our companies to declare permanent WFH. Waiting to visit a favorite restaurant, or to see yet another FOR LEASE sign. Waiting for the COVID case counts to fall or for a vaccine to arrive. Checking in on friends, and wondering whether we should get some extra toilet paper, just in case.

We're watching the lava-flow of democracy as people take to the streets and governments try to stop them all while waiting to find out if the world as we know it has changed and wondering whether we can or should go back. Even as events evolve and escalate, even when you've chosen a side, even when it's so clear that justice *can't wait,* it can sometimes feel like a holding pattern.

Everyone is just waiting.

We talked about the fog in the earliest days.[2] About how in crisis, it can be hard to make decisions because the facts on the ground keep changing. How as leaders, the fog fucks with our clarity. It makes us draw inward, and move more slowly. And it means we're late to deliver on the things our team needs to keep going.

The fog, for the most part, has lifted. Many of us are able to see clearly. And what we can see is water. Water to the north. To the south. To the east. To the west. We are clear, but we are adrift and there is no dry land in sight. And when we try to make sense of it, either through case counts or ICU capacity, or trying to guess what local school boards might do, we come up short. Not because we lack formal training as epidemiologists, hospital administrators, or civil servants, but because those people don't have answers either. At least not yet.

Water, all around. Paired with an urgent need to *act,* but also the knowledge that there's no point in running yourself down in random directions. A bias toward action pays off if you guess right. But right now the stakes feel very high for getting it wrong. So you wait.

MAKING PROGRESS WHILE STANDING STILL

There's no one, universal way to cope with the wait. There can't be. Sometimes enduring the wait is as much as we can do. We distract ourselves from it with nonsense like trying to find a supply of Bold BBQ Doritos because anything heavier is too much.

But there is a practice we come back to over and over. Whenever we find ourselves in the wait. When there's quiet and we're not sure if it will last or if we have the energy to want to do something with it.

We run tapes.

We're not sure where we picked up the expression "run your tapes." Google is unhelpful on this subject (though it offers a trip down VHS memory lane). We suspect it was from sports, since every pro player regularly runs their tapes and their opponents' tapes. But we've learned from past conversations that it's not a phrase in common use. So: To *run the tapes* is to review past performance—yours or someone else's—to see what you can learn from it. To run, and rerun, the metaphorical or literal video tape.

A secret about the two of us is that we run the tapes constantly—our tapes, other people's tapes, any industry, any time period. We replay the decisions we make and the implications of those decisions. We see how other people have built, or busted, their own success and whether we'd have the wisdom or the courage to do any better.

The core of that tortured "10,000 hours to be an expert" research is not the raw time spent. It's that that time be spent in "deliberative practice." *Deliberate*: as a verb, not an adjective. Deliberative practice is running your tapes.

If we had one open-ended interview question to ask Serena, Barack, or Beyoncé, it would be the same: "How do you think about running your tapes?" We're confident they'd each have a good answer.

The wait gives you time to run those tapes. And when it's too much mental effort to run our own, we run others.

We ran Michael Jordan's tapes.[3] What stood out for us was not just Jordan's story, but the stories around him. You can see how Dennis Rodman and Steve Kerr run their tapes, and how Jerry Kraus seems not to. We ran Taylor Swift's tapes.[4] We ran Alexander McQueen's tapes.[5] Jay-Z has multiple albums devoted to running his own tapes.[6] We listened to those, too.

As tech leaders, we run some tapes more than others. Our industry has a culture of postmortems. We talk about learning organizations. We tell ourselves that if we stumble or trip along the way, it should be because of the hard technical challenges we're trying to solve, not because someone in QA forgot to test in right-to-left languages. We talk about "not making the same mistake twice."

Many folks know this tool, are familiar with it in a work context, but stop short of applying it inward. It's not comfortable to dig up all the old shit and sift through it for pattern or meaning. But if you can make space for it, this is where breakthroughs happen.

FACTS, CONTEXT, EMOTIONS, MEANING

It helps to have a bit of distance at first. Don't pick a tape for something that happened last week. You're too close to it. Pick something from your last job or from the first job you ever had, and start to rebuild the lattice, the structure of it. The ingredients are the same ones used in narrative-focused therapy: facts, context, emotions, meaning. Start with what happened and the context and feelings you had at the time. As you rebuild, layer in the context you now have—about the impact of those decisions, both near-term and long-term. And work through how you would approach the same situation, faced with it today. Is there any learning there?

As you get more practiced, it's easier to pick more modern tapes off the shelf. They don't need to be old because you're not clinging to the idea that you were right and your former boss was an asshole. Even if he totally was, it's not the point of this exercise. From this place of spaciousness, you get as close as you can to objectivity. They're still *your* tapes. You're still entitled to have a perspective and even some bias. But when athletes and performers run their tapes, they're specifically looking for the ways they can get better. If you spend time only on the highlight reel, you're missing the point.

There's a humility to it. You'll know you're into the good stuff when you start to see your own mistakes, or see that you would not have made the call that someone else did and their call was better—not from a place of self-loathing, but from a place of self-knowledge. You'll know that you're into the good stuff when you start to see places you wouldn't make a mistake that someone else did—not from a place of self-satisfaction, but from a place of deliberateness.

The result of running tapes—especially your own—is that you accumulate all these places where you can now see around corners and make smarter choices. From the outside, people often attribute that change to wisdom or experience or "instinct." But that belies the hard, effortful work happening under the surface. You can be old and can have lived through a lot of shit and still be making the same mistakes.

Run your tapes. It's how you get ready for whatever comes after the wait.

· 12 ·

Just Because You Have Wi-Fi Doesn't Mean You're Connected

AUGUST
12
2020

[CW: This post talks about food. It does so as a metaphor, and not from a disordered or body image place, but if food talk is a thing that is hard for you, we wanted you to know up front.]

Last weekend we were talking with our big kid about food. She has declared that she wants to run a restaurant, and waves us off when we tell her they are very hard to run well. To be fair, we've never run one either.

We answer her questions about nutrients and calories. But we push back. "Food isn't just nutrients and calories, though, kiddo." We talk about reductive nutritionism. We talk about how it can be unhelpful and unhealthy to break food down into its constituent elements. Important things get lost along the way. We tell her that a good strategy for avoiding that loss is to eat real food—basic, recognizable, unreduced, unoptimized food. Neither of us grew up in houses that talked about this stuff in depth. And from a place of not knowing, it's hard to know what you're missing.

A few days later we were catching up with the owners of a phenomenal office design company, the people who built out RSG HQ. We've known them for more than a decade, and when it was time for us to build out our space, there was no one else we even called. They get, in a deep way, how important it is to build livable space. That you can buy cool lights and cool furniture and cool signage and still have a hollow, inhuman space. When we were planning our move, they insisted we have live plants because "if you can't grow plants, you can't grow people."

And when you talk to them, you have this sense that they want to scream. Flexible work is a wonderful thing, but everywhere they look they see people trying to put in a workweek in spaces that don't support it. Cramped home offices, dining room tables. Bathrooms. The passenger seat of the car. Yes, technically, you have Wi-Fi and a place to put a laptop and headphones. You have the ingredients you need to work. But so many important things are getting lost along the way.

It's like we're socially malnourished. This diet of Zoom and Slack and email gives you the appearance of a complete workplace, but it isn't complete. There's enough nutrition there to keep us going, but not enough for us to feel healthy. Not for all of us, anyhow. Some folks are getting what they need and having their remote work glow-up during pandemic. But others are finding the whole thing, well, tremendously difficult. It shows.

Like those stats you read (well, up in Canada, anyhow) about how half the population walks around chronically vitamin D deprived, we're seeing the accumulated effects of six months of global social anemia.

EAT WHEN YOU'RE HUNGRY

The global pandemic workday is 48 minutes longer.[1] Did you read that? Back in April there was U.S.-specific data suggesting folks were picking up an extra three hours a day.[2]

When you're dealing with a vitamin D deficiency, the remedy is to go get some, not to stay inside for another 48 minutes and 1.4 emails. You have people on your teams who are starved for a thing that Zoom calls aren't giving them: unpaid, unforced, joyful human connection.

It's not enough just to notice that your people are hungry. We're seeing a lot of HR teams shoving food at their people like the elderly grandma who lives next door. You look hungry. Eat. Eat. You look tired. Why don't you take a vacation? If you have grandparents who do this, you already know the deeply engrained reaction. You put one hand over your stomach and one hand up in the air and say, I'm okay. Really.*

The desire of the HR team to feed the people in their organizations comes from a good place. And they're right, of course.[3] We're all walking around hungry and tired. And leave it to the people in charge of people to notice first.

But it falls flat because the people on the receiving end know three important things. And as a boss, you'd be wise to take note.

1. **They feel lucky to have a job.** However tired they are, however weary, your people all know someone—a spouse, a parent, a friend—who got laid off at the start of all of this and is still trying to land on their feet.
1. **They want to keep the job they've got.** Yes, it's likely that your engagement surveys show happy worker bees buzzing away. And it's possible that that's spot on, but it brings us to the third point...
2. **They are unreliable narrators.** From that mix of exhaustion and gratitude and uncertainty, your people come back to

the tool they've been deploying this whole time. They tell you they're fine and hope you don't ask too many follow-up questions.

Quietly, we talk about the other reason people don't want to take a vacation or prioritize downtime. It's not because they don't need one. They do. It's because of the precariousness of **looks around** everything. The idea of zeroing out a balance of required-by-law vacation payout to sit at home when we're already sitting at home seems foolish. The rationale is based in a scarcity mindset,[4] and it goes something like this: In the event that I find myself without a job, well, I'll have plenty of time to sit at home then.

Our people know what they're supposed to do to feel better, to avoid burnout, to invest in their own resilience. And they're not doing it.

This isn't meant to make you paranoid. It's meant as a gentle nudge to the bosses and people leaders to think about how you design, given the constraints of the moment. Your old vacation system was likely pull-based, where people put in a request when they needed time off. A redesign might look more push-based, where we shut the office to extend a long weekend. Or we deploy something like summer hours to normalize downtime even if people aren't going anywhere.

We're not going to chastise people into taking care of themselves, but we can think about how to make our people feel safer doing so. How to give them room to do it without needing to ask permission or feeling like it's an indulgence that other people on the team aren't taking. How to lighten workloads so that our team members don't dread time off because of the pileup waiting for them next Monday.

Work can't really feed the social absence that we're all feeling. But work can give everyone more explicit room to feed themselves. As bosses, that's a thing we can do right now.

· 13 ·

Cheerful Swearing for a Change

AUGUST
26
2020

Last month we started work with several groups of managers, the first ones to go through our new, fully remote management program, Blueprint. We were excited, and terrified.

Not about the program itself. We worked *hard* on that. Every night for May and June we would get the kids to bed and then unpack all the recording gear. We'd record one 20- to 30-minute block after another. Compensation strategy. Giving hard feedback. Running a meeting your colleagues won't hate. Block after block. Night after night. That's stuff we know, though. We weren't worried about that.

The thing we worried about was whether anyone would come along. Like, there's a pandemic going on, right? And *we* think management topics are as vital as ever. But would *they*? We worried that no one would do the work. That they'd show up for the live calls and sort of coast through the rest of it. Not because they are lazy—most of the bosses we work with are trying their damnedest—but because they're *tired.* We're all *tired.* Every week that goes by, we find new depths of *tired.*

We worried they'd be too tired to come along. And we were completely wrong.

These groups have some of the most engaged and lit-up bosses we've ever worked with. When we tell you they are in it, they are *in it.* In our Q&A sessions, and in our inboxes between sessions. They are grappling with real shit. They are doing the work. They are *devouring* the work.

What the hell?

It took us a few weeks to figure out what was going on because everything else we expected is true. They *are* tired. They're drawing inward, focused more on their own team and less on the company as a whole. They're playing it safe and not raising some hard topics they know they should. That's all true.

But there is an appetite there. For clarity. For something that feels like answers. For a sense of forward motion and progress when they feel like they've been treading water. There's something about this moment we're in that makes growth and change and possibility deeply energizing for people. And once we realized that, we started to see it everywhere.

TRANSFORMATION IS IN THE AIR

Maybe you're tired of hearing about all the change. It's possible that you are full up on articles about the death of the office or Zoom wedding ceremonies. We don't blame you. There have been so many hot takes over the past few months. Hell, your open tabs probably contain contradictory hot takes. One announcing how we're all face-muting now followed by 15 virtual scavenger hunts you can run to onboard new employees. It's exhausting. You don't need another hot take, and we're in no mood to write one.

What we will offer—what someone, anyone, should bring to the conversation—is a coolly optimistic take:

There has never been a time when people were more ripe for change. You have an entire world tilted sideways. And the optimistic part is that you can only get transformation when people are receptive to change.

Humans are tricky. We hold on to a narrative about ourselves way longer than it's useful if it's comfortable. And in service of our own comfort, we cling to outdated narratives about other people. That comfort comes at a price, whether we're doing it to ourselves or to others. It is in comfort that we talk ourselves into staying in the wrong job, the wrong apartment, the wrong relationships. It is how we pressure friends and family to stay in the box we've put them in—all from a place of dodging disruption and staying comfortable.

But discomfort? Disruption? Well, we get those fuckers for free in 2020. You can't dodge them, and neither can the people holding on to an old version of you.

We are at an all-time low on stability and comfort. That's not a good thing or a silver lining. That's a tragedy so big it's hard to hold it in your head. And still, there is an opportunity there. The voices demanding that you stay the same—your own and others'—don't get to have that right now. None of us get to have that right now. But what we do have, each of us, is a once-in-a-lifetime opportunity to throw away the old story and tell a new one.

That doesn't have to look like management training for you. It doesn't even have to be a story about work, though we know that for many of you it is. But we told you at the start: transformation is in the air. There are *loads* of other places to find opportunities for change. It can be small adjustments to how you show up for your friends, family, and community. Checking in on people. Tipping well. Finding patience while waiting in line to get groceries.

Maybe you've got some baggage you can get rid of, now that none of us are traveling anyway. Or maybe you've just been meaning to try a thing. We hope you will. And we hope you'll let us know how it goes. Because what we're hearing is that after all the waiting,[1] some forward progress feels really fucking good.

· 14 ·

262,800 Minutes

SEPTEMBER
9
2020

"It's hard to meet anyone."

It's been six months since the lockdowns started here, and we're on a FaceTime call with our niece. She's in the States and has already started virtual school. They're two weeks into classes and she says all they've done so far are icebreakers. We feel for the teachers. They are trying to build cohesion for a group of kids most of whom have never met in person.

Her observation echoes. **It's hard to meet anyone.** And the accompanying one: **All we do are icebreakers.**

Last week, the *New York Times* had a piece about how our social skills are atrophying.[1] To be fair, before it was in the *NYT*, we wrote about it in a newsletter[2]—the idea that we're hungry for a core aspect of our humanity. Yes, at work, but also in general.

We look at it through the lens of work 'cause that's where we spend a lot of our brain cycles. The *Times* writer interviewed people who specialize in the impacts of isolation, from prison and solitary confinement to military deployments and remote field research.

Those experts said a thing that cut deep. We're both introverts. We like downtime and quiet and sitting still on the couch. Remember those early pandemic memes? The ones that noted how, for the introverts, a little bit less socializing might not be such a bad thing after all?

Introverts aren't immune to the social atrophy described in the piece. In fact, we're the most susceptible to the long-term impact of social isolation. The people who recognize that they are missing social interactions and seek them out tend to fare better. The ones who go inward have a much harder time reintegrating as socialization resumes.

Tucked in the middle of the article is a sentence that sounds remarkably similar to the conversation with my niece:

"Many of us have not met anyone new in months."

What's the opposite of social distance? It's not social closeness. It's social spontaneity—serendipitous moments of inspiration and collaboration. Those happen most when humans are in close proximity to other humans.

To bring it back to work, that social spontaneity is a core ingredient to our ability to be creative, generative, and innovative. If you're finding it harder to access that toolkit right now, it's because a key ingredient is missing.

Waiting it out isn't an option, which means there's a set of things that need to jump to the top of our to do list right now.

STEP ONE: YOU CAN'T REBUILD IN A BURNING BUILDING

Six months in, there is already serious damage to reckon with. No one, not one single person on the planet, has had a normal year. And it's going to mess with your team's ability to be socially spontaneous.

So. Back in April we told you to get proactive, to find out what mental health supports and programs were available to your team and then to bring them up in every one-on-one.

It's time to do that again. Not with the people you think need them—with everyone. Everyone needs mental health, and you want to aim for 100% coverage here. Some folks are very good at concealing their struggle, and many worry about stigma. It's so easy to say, "We're six months in, so this week I'm reminding everyone about these resources we offer."

And on top of the difficulty we're all having, some of your people are carrying another load. The racial justice protests that started in the spring haven't stopped. Neither has police violence toward Black people. In June your Black employees saw you post #BLM on social media, and commit to changes in your company. A question to ask yourself, now that it's September, is this: Is that work still happening? When was the last update to the team? Now that the media has moved on (even as the marches—and the murders—continue), it's on us as leaders to show that Black lives still matter.

Human relationships need safety and trust. That's step one.

STEP TWO: REMEMBERING HOW TO BE OUR BEST SELVES

Some of the companies we work with are lucky enough to be growing during all this. In a few cases, almost half the company are post-COVID hires, people who live in the same city but have never met their coworkers—people who applied, interviewed, received an offer, accepted, celebrated, and onboarded during lockdown.

In normal times, this describes any remote worker. But in normal times the rest of us can make the effort to pull that person in. In normal times we'd understand how isolating it can be to be both new and at a distance. It might still feel awkward, but we'd send some "welcome" emojis in Slack and suggest a quick call to help them get situated. We wouldn't feel so depleted that the idea of another Zoom call with a stranger made us want to cry. In normal times we'd have been our best selves.

Few of us feel like we have the energy to be our best selves right now. But as a boss you still have a job to do. The pandemic is not this person's fault. They draw motivation from the same stuff we all do, and a key element of that is our relationships.[3] It's not your job as a boss to be everyone's friend, but it is your job to set the people in your organization up for success.

That job doesn't stop with the new hires, either. Hands up if you've found that you're keeping your head down more these days, if you're focused more on your own team's work and less on what other people are up to. Isolation and siloing are natural responses to being overwhelmed. They don't make you a bad person. But if the team is going to unclench their teeth[4] and relax their shoulders, many of them will need you to go first.

As a boss you have more of the context that your team needs. You're in different meetings; you have different access. But many bosses have stopped using that access. They've been in their own protective isolation silos, and it's time to get back out of them. Your team needs you investing in cross-team relationships again. They need you to have broader situational awareness again, so you can reduce unpleasant surprises because you're in more conversations and have a more complete picture.

And this will mean more awkward Zoom calls. Some of you will be rebuilding muscle that has atrophied more than you realized. It will be surprising how *weird* you feel talking to people. You may rush to finish the calls early just for the relief of hanging up.

Keep going. It will get better. And you will feel more like your best self. Or at least more...normal. Because it's been way too long.

· 15 ·

How to Quit Your Job During a Pandemic

SEPTEMBER
23
2020

We should start by saying that not all of us need to quit our jobs. That would be quite disruptive.

Disruptive in the deeply individual sense, where quitting means turning off income and benefits and a source of social interaction in the midst of a global pandemic, at a time when income and benefits and social interaction are scarce.

And disruptive in the global sense. We cannot all rage-quit this week or massive elements of our world would grind to a halt. Food and medicine and school and (non-essential but still oh-so-essential) management training all rely on us showing up.

We're hearing from more folks who know they need to quit, who have held out for as long as they could but who can't do it indefinitely. People write us to say the last few newsletters have cut close, that they see themselves in the discussions around burnout and unsustainable work habits. And they reach out because the space between knowing it's time to quit and actually quitting feels overwhelming. They need help figuring out how to do it.

If you don't need to quit during a pandemic, this one isn't for you. The rest of you who are still here, welcome.

This is the unofficial guide for how to quit your job during a pandemic.

STEP ONE: PICK A DATE

How long do we have? We talking hours? weeks? months? years? We can build a plan around any of those, but the timeline will inform everything else. So the first step is figuring out when you plan to quit.

It's common to struggle with this question. Even when you know you need to quit, nailing it down feels impossible. But like many things in life, you can use sliders to figure it out.[1] Do you still expect to be working there in a year? Is your work unsafe, unhealthy, or creating an urgent need for you to leave immediately?

Most folks who are planning to quit aren't talking hours. And once they've decided to move on, many folks experience physical discomfort at the idea of putting in another year.

Pick an actual date. Not a month, not a season, not a rough gesturing. A date. Like one that a human person could have been born on.

Not because we say so, but because a date brings a bunch of things into focus. Once we know when we want to be out, we can build a workback plan. If you know your last day, you can figure out when you need to talk to your boss. In many places you're only required to give two weeks' notice. But this is a global pandemic, and your boss might need more than two weeks.

A WORD ABOUT LONG GOODBYES

If two weeks feels unspeakably short and you have a good relationship with your boss and trust them not to flip out, you can talk to them sooner. You can choose to give more notice. But be careful:

Everyone overestimates how long it will take them to wind up—and underestimates the discomfort of staying once the news is out.

We have both done long exec transitions, partly from not wanting to let our CEOs down and partly from genuinely caring about the orgs and wanting to leave them in a good spot. Those are lovely things. But once your team knows you're leaving, they stop giving you new work, and your calendar clears up pretty fast.

So get yourself to a last date, and a date when you plan to tell your boss. Even without being on the other side of the hard conversation, the process of picking dates helps a lot of folks feel lighter. It shakes off some of the weight of knowing you need to quit but feeling stuck. You can't control the pandemic, but you *can* start to make decisions even while the future is unclear. The pandemic can be out there pandemicing, but after that date, you no longer have to remember your login credentials.

STEP TWO: THAT SHAME FEELING

There's this push–pull thing that happens in your head when you start to think about leaving, though. Not for everyone, but for enough people that we have to talk about it.

At first the idea of leaving, the *clarity* of leaving, is so appealing. You get a date, you write a plan. It feels like relief when you hold it in your head—to be able to put it all down.

But the closer you get to that plan—the more it becomes a concrete thing with some next steps—the more new anxieties appear. You usually feel it in your stomach, and it feels like shame.

There are generally two piles of stomach-shame feelings at work. You may have one, both, or neither.

One kind feels like *"The people I work with will have to carry the stuff that I put down. And they're fried, too."* Or, sometimes, *"My boss has actually been really good throughout this and I can't do this to them right now."* The abandonment shame.

The other kind feels like *"I don't have a new job lined up yet. It's irresponsible to leave this one without finding something new."* The recklessness shame.

If you let them, these feelings will put you right back where you started. They'll push you off your dates. You'll be back at *"I need to quit, but I can't."*

TAKING CARE OF YOURSELF IS NOT ABANDONMENT

The thing to understand about the shame of abandoning your team is that it's absolutely true. Yes, when you leave, your work will fall to other people. And yes, they may be running at their own burnout redline. Those things could be true. So now what?

There's a beauty to solidarity. Standing with our colleagues is how we protect the most vulnerable among us and agitate for change. It's a way to lend our strength to other people. But when you've got no strength left, it's okay to protect yourself, too.

Whether it's tomorrow, or next month, or ten years from now, at some point, if you're ever going to leave this job, your work will fall to other people. That's not a reason to never leave. It's a reason to write the transition plan while you still have the energy to do it well.

TAKING CARE OF YOURSELF IS NOT RECKLESS

As for the recklessness shame, well, there's no general answer to that one. Everyone's money situation is different, and we are not here to tell you to "chase your dreams" into debilitating credit-card debt. Maybe you really do need to gate your entire plan on finding something new. It's not our place to tell you otherwise.

We can tell you the true thing, though. The true thing is that you're too fried to be creative about what the next thing ought to be. That you need real *time*—months, probably—to recover from this thing before you start that thing. That it would be healthy to start from a place of "how might we design my departure so that I have that time?"

It's at least worth doing some work in a spreadsheet to see how long you could go if you had to. You might have to. The quitting might not wait that long. And it will help you to know what's what, anyway.

Our experience is that the stomach-shame feelings tend to fade in the face of a plan that anticipates them.

THAT CONVERSATION

Bosses, we told you months ago to expect turnover.[2] That people would hang on as long as possible but that many of them were starting to get crispy. And how they kept repeating the same mantra: *I'm lucky. I'm fortunate. I'm grateful. So many other people would be happy to be in my place right now.*

Maybe you thought we were overplaying that hand, that *your* teams would be spared. Maybe they will be. But if someone comes into your next one-on-one ready to have That

Conversation, well, we're sorry. We've been there, and it's no fun, even during a normal year.

You can do all the standard things as a boss. You can try to negotiate. You can try to reallocate workloads or fast-track the promotion you've been sitting on. Just remember what's behind that decision right now. Remember that you may be looking at someone at the end of a dozen rounds of burnout and stomach-shame feelings trying to take care of themselves.

And if you're the one bringing this conversation to your boss, if you're the one quitting, we feel for you, too. We're here if we can help. And we hope you'll get some rest.

· 16 ·

Companies Don't Make Decisions—People Do

OCTOBER
7
2020

There's a thing happening right now that doesn't make sense.

There's a global pandemic. No one has felt safe for months. The layoffs in the spring were massive, and many people's jobs have not come back. So you can understand why those who still have work would count their blessings and keep their heads down. They might not like it. They might have concerns about the work. But you would understand if they decided to shut up and dribble. You might even expect it.

Only they aren't.

In our own networks, and in the world at large, we're seeing the opposite. Despite the precarity of work, despite the uncertainty of what the fall will mean for COVID, we're seeing people, often very junior people, voting with their feet. When their employer is out of step with their values, they are organizing walkouts. They are leaking to the press. They are unionizing workplaces that never expected to be unionized. They are protecting themselves, and they are protecting each other. And they are quitting.

If it seems like we've written a lot about quitting in the newsletter lately, this is why. It's not just that people are quitting their jobs during a pandemic. It's that they're quitting their jobs during a pandemic *because of values*. That's a hell of a thing.

This isn't a newsletter about quitting. It is a newsletter about work. Under the most precarious conditions, people are renegotiating their relationship to their work. That's important.

REPPIN' HARD FOR THE STATUS QUO

While junior folks are organizing for social change, something very different is happening in the C-suite. This summer has seen a parade of CEOs trying hard to pretend that social change is something that happens somewhere else. *Anywhere* else.

Three months ago, every corporate social media account was posting that Black lives matter. Every employee book club was reading Dr. Kendi.[1] A question for any organization that steps into work like this is, "Those words are important, but where will we see it backed up with policy and action?" And faced with the hard work necessary to dismantle systemic oppression, several CEOs have decided to stick with the status quo.

Coinbase's CEO declared his company "apolitical."[2] He says that he thinks of his company as a professional sports team—paying no attention, it seems, to how actual professional sports teams have responded to social justice issues. He gave people a week to take severance if they disagree.

Hootsuite (a fucking B Corp!)[3] formed a committee to chew on whether to take a contract helping ICE with their social media. They said yes. And then, after an employee put herself on the line to tweet about it,[4] reversed course.

And, of course, there's always Shopify. Tobi Lütke's platform funds every alt-right, white supremacist group clever enough to keep overt hate speech off of their coffee mugs.[5] Rumor has it that they too have a "some employees may quit because of our stance, and that's okay" internal policy. Cool cool cool.

So on the one hand, you have employees agitating for a more complete view of how their employers' activities impact the world. And on the other, you have CEOs hoping that no one will notice those impacts. And the thing that jumps out to us is that there's something missing.

Where are the bosses in this story? Where are the layers between the employees' sense of moral integrity and their CEOs' lack of it?

THE OLD RULES

In the world of leadership development, most people want to work with the CEO, in part because of a dated assumption: that working at the tippy-top is how you make change within organizations. It happens in the C-suite and flows downhill. The role of managers was to execute on and operationalize the vision, to take the decisions and put them into practice, regardless of their personal opinions or perspective. "We're not paying you," the argument went, "for your feelings."

But these days, holy shit are we paying you for your feelings. We're paying you for your storytelling. We're paying you for your ability to keep a highly skilled workforce motivated and engaged. We're paying you to develop and grow people. And we're paying you to take the vision and tailor it—to build a personalized version of how that vision connects to the day-to-day work of every person on your team.

Once demand for skilled workers outpaced supply, the distribution of power shifted. Tech became a place where employers had to compete for, attract, and retain talent. And as research piled up showing that engaged employees outperform, tech CEOs started to care a lot about catered lunches and feelings.

But they still expected employees to leave their politics at the door.

Those CEOs were wrong. They were playing a new game by old rules—ones that assumed they still held all the power.

THE NEW RULES

There's only one group of people within an organization that gets to apply bidirectional pressure. CEOs push down. Individual employees push up. Only bosses do both. You can't make real and lasting change in an organization without the middle.

The middle is a hard place to be in 2020. When the decisions of the company don't make sense, we need you to say so. Your job isn't to mindlessly push these decisions onto your team. The psychological safety you build exists so that your people can tell you when things aren't okay. It's a scary thing to say "I don't want my labor supporting an organization that forces refugees to have hysterectomies." When people do, we need you pushing that concern up.

And not in a one-sided way, either. As a team, we need you to hold us accountable to the work we signed up to do, too. A boss who always agrees with their team is a liability. Work is not summer camp. Questions of morality are one thing, but we've seen teams derailed over everything from technology choices to seating arrangements. As a boss, sometimes you'll need to break the tie and make a call that some of us won't like.

Making those calls is the job. If you make bad ones often enough, you should get out of the seat. But while you're in it, they're yours to make. That's what we're paying you for. For every company being dragged into the spotlight by their own employees, it's worth asking: What you would do as that person's boss?

In all of it, your job is to be the translation layer. And it's a really hard job, because you have to constantly juggle the needs of the business and the needs of your team, and every decision you make risks pissing off one group or another. But that's not an excuse to avoid making decisions.

We're leaving the most junior and least privileged to step forward as the ethical guardrails of our organizations. That should be us—not because we have all the answers, but because the people on our teams trust us. We hold their employment relationship with the organization. And when we disappoint our teams, it's not nameless or faceless. The people in charge will listen to us. Because when they disappoint us, that's not nameless or faceless either.

We don't need you to have all the answers. But if you're sitting in the seat, we need you asking the hard questions. We need you listening, and acting on what you hear. And if you get to the point where you're in an ethically compromising situation and you can't make change or can't be heard, well… We already wrote the one about quitting.[6]

· 17 ·

Is It Okay If I Eat While We Talk?

OCTOBER
21
2020

A few weeks ago, we set up an appointment to put the snow tires on the car. We try to do it early. There's always this giant rush as soon as the first leaves change color. In Canada, snow reserves the right to show up in October and stick around until May.

And then last week, sitting at lunch, we realized. We just... didn't do it. We'd called ahead the night before to make sure the tires were in. And then that morning we just entirely failed to show up. Or even notice that we hadn't. For days.

When we finally called them back to (re-)schedule, we had to start from that place you do when you're not sure if you dreamed something. "I think we had an appointment to switch tires. Did... Did we have that and just not do it?"

We knew what we needed to do. We just didn't do it.

Maybe you have your snow tires all sorted. But everywhere we've looked for the last few weeks, we've seen variations on the same thing.

Bosses, frustrated that their teams are missing steps. And not in a postmortem "Let's unpack this and carry the learning forward across the org" sort of way. They're pointing to sloppy errors, not new lessons we haven't learned yet. These are core truths about how our work or industry operates—ones we're just failing to put into practice even though we know better.

We're also hearing from lots of folks that they're forgetting to eat. It's happening in our work with bosses. People join Zoom calls midway through a sandwich and mumble, "Sorry, I didn't have time to eat." We're talking to HR leaders who turn off the video at the start of the call. "Is it okay if I eat while we talk?" More people tell us they are surviving on granola bars and coffee because the flow of their workday doesn't make space for anything else. They know better. And yet.

There's so much about COVID that is new and scary and requires creative adaptability. But what's messing everyone up seven months in is stupid shit. Systemically, we aren't tripping over new and unfamiliar obstacles; we're tripping over our shoelaces.

IT'S NOISY IN THERE

We're asking our brains to do a lot of work right now. We're doing our day jobs, caretaking, feeding ourselves, figuring out voting, trying to keep track of the latest public health guidelines, R (and also *k*)[1], and waiting for updates from the vaccine trials.[2] It's. A. Lot.

And in the face of all that noise, our brains are doing something very clever. They're dropping some stuff on the floor. Unfortunately, a lot of what's ending up on the floor is the stuff that's not so cognitively intense. It's not the COVID-tracking, it's the life-tracking.

And it's why we all feel like the stuff we're screwing up is the stuff where we ought to know better. Because we *do* know better—there's just not enough space to keep it all in the air.

One of us lives with ADHD. And the other of us lives with someone living with ADHD. And the thing about a brain that often misses details or forgets birthdays is that minor fuck-ups hit different.

Lots of ADHD folks live with a compounding story about these moments. If this is how you keep score, every one of these stumbles can kick off a cycle of shame and frustration, and that shame and frustration can make it harder to get back on top of things. From that place, the story about being a fuck-up becomes a self-fulfilling prophecy.

Everyone has these moments. You don't need a diagnosis to flake on a seasonal tire appointment. And maybe for you, that missed appointment is a standalone. You're able to shrug it off and move on. But for a lot of folks right now, it's further proof that they are a hot mess. And it doesn't matter that everyone else is a mess, too.

It takes work to change the hot mess narrative, to track and celebrate the wins rather than beat yourself up over every miss. And particularly as bosses, you not only hold that narrative for yourself, you hold it for your team.

THE SECRET TO JUGGLING

As individuals, the answer to all of this is so obvious it feels like a bad joke. The way to get back on top of things is to do the things you already know you should do. Rest. Unplug. Breathe. Remember to eat.

Make lists, if you're a list maker. Use technology to remind you of the things on those lists. Pilots don't use checklists because they're forgetful; pilots use checklists because they're professionals and because it is far better—and safer—to have a checklist carry that mental load.

As a boss, understand that your people are all in this. They may not be tripping over their shoelaces today, but we promise they're dropping balls somewhere. They'd have to be. And some of them are feeling shitty about it.

Your job is not to make it so no balls ever drop. Your job is to choose which ones.[3] If you refuse to choose, it doesn't mean nothing drops. It means you have no insight into which ones drop, in which order, until it's too late. And the longer you wait, the more unsteady everything gets.

If your team can only get one thing done this quarter, what's the one to focus on? And do they know it? You might get away with asking for more than that. But when you add something new, it puts extra risk on every other ball in the air.

The mistakes happening right now don't come from stupidity or indifference or malice. If you assume that they do, you will make bad management decisions. Your people don't need a lecture about things they already know how to do. They don't need more shame about feeling like a fuck-up. The more you overload them, the less effective they'll be.

Your people are trying their best even when it seems like they aren't. Even when it seems like they're sloppy, or checked out. If they're fucking up, it's because everything is harder right now.

Manage from the assumption that your people need to put down a few balls as gently, but quickly, as they can and that they need your help figuring out which ones can drop. Manage from the assumption that they may not have eaten for a while.

· 18 ·

Read This First

NOVEMBER
4
2020

[This newsletter came out the morning after the U.S. presidential election in which Joe Biden ultimately prevailed, ousting Donald Trump as president. On this Wednesday morning, though, the best anyone could say was that it was too close to call.]

Did you get much sleep?

Our dual-citizenship household did not. Even if you're not American, yesterday was an important day. At the end of a year of anxiety and suffering—like, an entire year of grimace emojis 😬—the question of which way the U.S. goes is momentous. As we write this, it's not obvious which way it went. At least not yet.

So we're back in the fog.[1] Not from the shock of a global pandemic—this one was a fog we could see rolling in months in advance. But predicting the fog doesn't give you any more ability to see through it once it arrives.

In the fog, simple helps. So we're keeping it short: three things our boss people need to do this week, regardless of where the pieces land.

1. FIND SOME BURST CAPACITY

The rest of this week is going to require burst capacity. Take a look at your calendar and imagine a bucket of water. Every existing thing on your calendar is an amount of water in the bucket. Staring down a wall of seven-minute Zoom meetings? We're gonna call that 100% full. Anywhere you see empty space, that's your burst capacity. And our sense is that you're going to need more of it than usual.

You don't need to completely clear the decks. We're not saying dump the bucket upside down and cancel all your meetings. But you do need to make space in case something crash lands. Aim for at least 30% capacity. Push the nonurgent things to next week or beyond so that when you're ready if the unexpected comes up.

And if you're wondering what the heck might crash-land, that brings us to point number two.

2. EXPECT THAT YOUR PEOPLE MIGHT BE RAW

Bosses, you are gonna get this one wrong. And it's not your fault. But this is us flagging it for you.

Some of your team finds comfort in work. They might be the same people who told you so back in March—that when the world turned upside down, it was reassuring to slot into work. Because it was familiar. Because it gave them something to do. Because it felt like a port of calm when so much was out of control.

Some of your people are just so fucking done right now. They are on the heels of eight months in an unending stress position and they *cannot even*. They have been doomscrolling a lot. They are working from home, sometimes in small spaces, often alone. And for many, it's been months since anyone gave them a hug. They are not okay.

As folks come online, you will have people who do not give a shit about politics and people who do but don't want to talk about it. And you'll have people who do and *do* want to talk about it. And the hard news for you is that you'll have no idea which is which. They aren't labeled with a Slack emoji, so you're gonna want to proceed with caution. They might be raw.

But you can help clear their schedules. Or give them more stuff to distract them, if that's what they need. You can listen for unusual levels of conflict or missed deadlines or workload stress. And you can choose not to attribute those things to underperformance when you hear them.

This is a week to reach for empathy before accountability—not because accountability doesn't matter, but because you're at risk of mistaking hurt humans for bad employees. That's a mistake we don't want you to make.

3. LEAD

We need you to lead. And maybe we need that every day but *especially* today. We need you to connect the dots, see us where we are, and remind us that there's meaning to the work we do. Easier said than done, we know. But if you're not sure how to start, here's a template:

- **First, acknowledge what's happening in the world.** In an email, in a team Slack channel, whatever makes sense. A hard part for many people is knowing whether they can talk about it at all.

- **Remind everyone of the supports available.** If time off is an option. If deferring deadlines is an option. If you have benefits that support mental health. If you're able to open up office hours or just be in an open call for people to drop in. You can't accurately predict who will need these reminders, so give them to everyone.
- Last, and this is the hardest part: **Give us a sense that you get it.** And, ideally, that the company does, too. This is the hardest because you might not, or the company might not, and it won't help to fake it. But if you do, we need to hear that. Companies are made of people,[2] and it matters a lot to know whether those people get it or not.

This fog will lift. But while we wait for the fog to lift, expect to drive a little slower, and take a little more care.

· 19 ·

But We're Being Really Careful

NOVEMBER
18
2020

At some point every psych student hears about the dam. You'll be talking about some concept—denial, probably—and your prof will say, "Have we talked about the towns by the dam yet?"

The problem with dams is that sometimes they fail. And when a dam fails, the results for anyone downstream are catastrophic. So a fun thing for psychologists to do is survey the people who live in the shadow of the dam. They call them up and ask them, in essence, "How freaked out are you about the dam?"

The towns 50 miles out are aware of it. The ones 30 miles downstream worry. By 10 miles out, they're terrified.

And the towns two miles from the dam? The ones whose lives will be violently washed away if the dam fails? Well, they consistently tell the pollsters that they aren't worried at all.

Like any good parable, it doesn't make sense except that it does. Because how else could you function? With that kind of fear literally looming over your home in the middle distance, you'd have to shut it out, wouldn't you? After a few months of living in terror of this thing, you'd have to give yourself some kind of excuse to not think about it, to convince yourself that it's not actually a risk. How else could you endure, right?

It's not just dams breaking. Pilots underestimate risks that would prevent an on-time landing. Investors underestimate risk of loss. People who have *personally survived* major tornadoes *still* underestimate tornado risk.[1]

And we're in the middle of a global pandemic. We know now that the virus spreads though the air. Particularly if people are unmasked. Particularly indoors. But there's stuff we want to do—indoor, unmasked stuff that we really want to do.

And we've found a way to help us stop worrying about the dam.

VIRUSES DON'T HAVE CHEAT CODES

Way back in March, we started every cancellation email with "Out of an abundance of caution..." By November nothing about those emails seems abundantly cautious. "Out of a modicum of prudence" is more accurate.

The retrospective here is interesting. We know so much more than we did, and yet our knowledge is what's fucking us. We know enough to recite the mantra of the past eight months. Our universal "Get out of jail free" card. The incantation, like three swift knocks on the nearest wood table.

Don't worry. We're being really careful.

Don't worry. It's just a backyard gathering. It's just e.[2] Everyone will be in masks. We're just getting a few people together for Thanksgiving. And all of them have been home, too. We'll only go indoors if someone has to pee. Or if it rains.

Our children's great-grandmother recently announced she was flying several states away to attend Thanksgiving. "Don't worry," she said. "I'll be wearing a mask on the flight." She's 95.

And from her perspective, she is being really careful. She's not going to raves. At least, we don't *think* she's going to raves. But even if she were, she'd be masked and have Purell, so we'd be right back to the start of our "being really careful" loop.

WHAT IT MEANS FOR WORK

Bosses, we can't fix all of this. The scale of the human miscalibration here is massive. And in most cases it steps outside of your lane as a boss to yell at your people for having their friends over.

But we should be doing everything we can to make it easier for our colleagues to make good choices. And when people's risk calculus is messed up, clear expectations are a gift. (Clear expectations, to be clear, are almost always a gift.)

IN THE OFFICE

Over the summer, a friend of ours was told to bring his team back into work. They were deemed essential, and everyone was told it was time to come in. But when they got to the warehouse, no safety adjustments had been made. It was business as usual.

He sent his team home. And then told HQ that he wouldn't call them back until it was safe, essential or otherwise. He went on to enumerate what "being really careful" would look like... in a bulleted list.

If you have people coming into the workplace, they have likely mastered "But we're being really safe." It's what they tell their parents. And partners. And kids. And loved ones. Your job as the boss is to make sure it's true. It's not to point to the sanitizer on the way into the building. It's to put in the time to understand local guidelines where you live and the best advice globally on safe workplaces, and to advocate loudly so that your team comes into the safest environment possible, or else not at all.

OUT OF THE OFFICE

Not everyone is calling people back to an office or a warehouse. A lot of teams have been home since spring and are staying home for the foreseeable future. It's insufficient to say, "Everyone is home; therefore, we're being really careful." Yes, it's cautious from an epidemiological point of view. But there are major mental and physical health implications to long-term isolation. Even with the vaccine news sounding cheerful right now, we're staring down several more months of this. And winter is coming for the northern hemisphere.

Being careful looks different for you WFH bosses, but we still need you. Think about the boss standing outside the warehouse with his team listing out the things that would need to be true for them to be safe inside. What does the list look like for *your* team? What do they need to work in isolation in a safer, healthier way?

You're likely somewhere in 2021 planning right now—either in the anxiety of not having started or in the frustration of trying to pretend you have a crystal ball coming out of this ridiculous year. As you write that plan, make sure it anticipates employee fatigue and depletion. This may show up in how you budget, how you set goals, how you manage performance. You ought to calibrate as though you have a workforce that's been home and going through this shit for eight months. Because you do.

Do your mental health benefits for your employees have annual caps on them? If people are hitting those caps, we need you to figure out how to lift that limit. Is your company setting goals that assume a 100% productive workforce? We need you in that room pushing for a 60% target in the first half even when it's embarrassing to be the one arguing for less stretch. No one should be at the gym right now anyhow—stretch is off the table.

Bosses, that's your job this week. Yes, take care of your people. That's always your job. But this week in particular we need you using your sway in the organization to make structural change. We need you managing up and across. Whatever's on that list is going to need action if your people and your organization are going to make it through winter in one piece.

You probably already know what emails you need to send.

· 20 ·

Evidence-Based Hope

DECEMBER
2
2020

Tony Hsieh died last week.

It's not our place to tell you who Tony was. Those stories should be told by people who knew him. Paul Carr and Sarah Lacy have written beautiful, complex goodbyes.[1] They are worth your time.

We didn't know him, but we certainly knew *about* him. We talk about Tony with the bosses we train—he's part of the organization design curriculum because during his time at Zappos, Tony became the world's most visible proponent of Holacracy.

Holacracy, if you haven't seen the word before, is a system for organizing a company without bosses. It's part of a movement that calls itself "self-management." They talk a lot about "teal organizations" ushering in a newer, more fulfilling way to work.

Tony went all-in. He offered Zappos managers new roles as individual contributors, or else the door. He organized the company into tiny independent "loops." Hundreds of employees quit in the ensuing confusion,[2] but he didn't let up. A more enlightened future of work is always going to have its skeptics, after all.

We won't do Holacracy justice here—it takes whole books to fully develop—but suffice it to say that we aren't fans. Intuitively, we're skeptical that you can erase deep power imbalances by playing games with the org chart. Empirically, it doesn't tend to work out well.[3] In fact it often ends up gaslighting your marginalized employees.[4]

Zappos eventually dropped Holacracy.[5] Even a guy like Tony couldn't wish it into working. But while the system of Holacracy seems hopeless, the message is a hopeful one. The message is that work can be better. That it can have dignity, and value, and fulfillment, and joy. That's a hopeful, important message in any time, but especially today. We don't have a quarrel with the hope. We just have a different point of view on how to get there.

IS THIS A MOMENT?

Last week, we were talking to a reporter. He's working on a piece about work. It's topic we love. And if you get us started, it's often hard to get us to stop.

When we start the call, he does not sound hopeful. He's writing about work before and after COVID. But of course, the after-COVID part is TBD. We have some guesses, but it's hard to know from late 2020 what office work in 2022 will feel like.

His core question is whether this is *a moment*—this middle spot we're in right now. **Are we in a once-in-a-lifetime position to address the worst parts of work from the before times? And build something better and more sustainable for the after times?**

We leaned so far into the phone to answer that our lower backs were sore after the call.

Yes. Yes! Yes, we can and should build something different. Yes, work can be so much better than it was. Yes, people should expect more. Yes, it is possible to have work that isn't abusive. No, burnout isn't inevitable. And OMG YES, so much of this is fixable.

And then he asks the money question—the one that gives away why he feels despondent while we are jumping over each other with excitement.

How do you know where to start? It's such a big, interrelated problem. How do you even begin?

And he's right. The individual boulders are enormous: the intersections of work and power and systematic oppression and burnout and isolation. We don't fault anyone for thinking they're hard to move. They are.

But lifting boulders isn't about the giganticness. It's not about moving the whole thing in one go. It's about finding the places where movement can happen—the water flowing above, below, eroding the soil, chipping away until the entire landscape shifts.

WE START WITH THE BOSSES

In the early days of writing The Co-pour, we got a lot of Holacracy folks following along and cheering. At first we were confused. It's strange for us to get kudos from a group that's committed to the end of bossing. Aren't we rooting for opposite sides? Our T-shirts say "competent management." Theirs say "no management." What gives?

Maybe you can already see what we couldn't...

The starting point for both teams is a strong rebuke of the status quo. Saying out loud that work isn't working. Screaming from the rooftops that humans cannot do creative and generative work without humanity and that to expect otherwise is a recipe for disappointment of the perpetual and soul-crushing variety.

Up to that point we all agree. But from there we diverge.

Bosses hold power. They control how work feels. Holacracy tries to fix this by getting rid of them. But that doesn't solve it because in a group of humans, you can't assert power away. You can erase the org chart, you can insist that everyone is equal, but all you actually do is make power less scrutable and accountable. When you do, you end up reinventing the same oppressive systems you were trying to tear down.

We talk about power head on, and what it means to be the people who control how work feels. What an awesome responsibility it is and what happens when leaders fall short. We don't let them pretend it away. We sit in the discomfort of the thing.

And that's where our hope comes from: because we watch them do it. We see bosses—first-time leads and seasoned executives—sit and fucking *grapple* with it. It's not comfortable for them. Sometimes they get frustrated or angry. Sometimes they cry. But they do the work. And we hear it from them. And we hear it from the people around them. And we hear it from the people they manage.

Hope rests on the belief that things can be different and that we have the agency to make that change. Our hope isn't foolish or naive or good only in theory. It's evidence-based. We're not despondent about the size of the big-ass rocks. We're hopeful because we've seen them move. Work can be better, and we already have the tools.

And a thing we're sitting with right now is that we wish we could show Tony what we're up to.

· 21 ·

It's Not Rest If You Can't Sleep

DECEMBER
16
2020

Yes, you have to set goals.

We know. This year has been an exercise in just how unknowable the future is. How humans make plans and COVID laughs. The futility of trying to make business objectives as the ground shifts beneath you and then shifts again as local and global regulations try to anticipate the next moves of an invisible enemy.

This week, the first vaccine doses have started to roll out across North America, though all the experts say we have a ways to go before we're back to office potlucks. In the wake of promising news, it's tempting to kick goal-setting farther down the road.

Let's see how it goes—keep doing what we're doing and pick it up once we know a bit more. After all, isn't now a good time to take a break?

The temptation to punt on goals is real. We understand why goal-setting feels impossible. But we need you to ignore the siren song of waiting it out.

In boring times, goals are a fundamental tool for organizational alignment and predictability. At the close of 2020, every boss we know would love to go shopping at the alignment and predictability store.

Goals are how you pay in cash for that alignment and predictability. You don't get one without the other. And if that makes you tired, this is the last thing we need from you before you go rest those weary bones.

PERFECT DOESN'T EXIST

Our kindergartener came home one day and said, "Perfect doesn't exist." She learned it at school. Teachers these days are super into growth-mindset stuff, and the idea of perfect gets in the way of kids' trying and failing—which is basically how anyone ever gets good at anything. When anyone in our house says "perfect," she pops up like a small, serious elf to remind us that "perfect doesn't exist."

Our gift to you this end-of-year planning season is in the form of this small, serious elf. If you're waiting for perfect strategy or perfect goals or perfect context, the elf is here to remind you: **Perfect doesn't exist.**

So why bother setting goals if there's no such thing as perfect? And if all our context is guaranteed to change?

Two reasons:

The first is that your people need clarity. Even if you don't know all of the details, chances are good you have some. And at the close of a year of uncertainty, anywhere you can illuminate things you ought to.

Annual goals are an opportunity to repeat the core truths of your business or to challenge them and tell a new story about what we're here to do and for whom. If you've been in the shit for the past ten months, goals are an invitation to pick your head up and look around.

The second is that your people need a win. Setting goals means we can mark progress. We have a way of stepping outside of the grind to say, "Hey, we did a thing"—and then giving a shove to celebrate.

All through the year, we've been talking to founders and CEOs. And we ask, how's it going? For many of them it's rough. But for others, their businesses are growing.[1] The pandemic accelerated a bunch of digitization in their industry and their biggest problem is keeping up with demand.

There's a concern around not wanting to tempt fate or appear boastful, but the result is that many teams haven't celebrated a win together in almost a year. Do you know how hard that is on morale? To have scrambled and pivoted and been successful at it only to find that there's a sign at the end of the race that says "26.2 more miles to go"?

It's no wonder so many people see that sign and want to lie down.

TOP DOWN, THEN BOTTOM UP

So, okay, maybe you can see the value of putting up wins for your team and the value of clarity. But leaders who can see the value of those things still often get hung up on the Right Way to author and communicate them. They're looking for perfect again. It's why, in our work, we see organizations adopt and abandon goals frameworks more than any other management tool.

We're not devout fans of any particular system, we're just fans of the stuff that works. And a core element of what works for goals is their directionality. Successful goals systems usually have a "top down, then bottom up" structure built in explicitly.

That means that goal-setting starts with the CEO. If you're a CEO reading this, we need you to get us going. Not because you're smarter than us, or more strategic than us, or some kind of wizard, but because it's what we're paying you to do. We're paying you to see the whole business and its place in the world. When there are things that keep you up at night, when there are things that you can see coming at a distance, we need you, in the simplest language you can find, to spell it out. What is make or break for our organization, and why?

The next step is for you to tell that story to the senior team. Help them understand where there are threats and where there are opportunities and why these are the most important things to get done. If you're a member of that senior team, we need you to do your job, too. The thing we pay you to do is to understand the needs of the organization, and then also figure out how to get your teams aligned to accomplish those things.

And then each senior leader goes and tells their team. And on it goes through the entire organization. But at every step, the storytelling is crucial. Bringing it back to existential questions and simple language is crucial. And if you're a boss in one of these meetings, your job is to ask questions until you understand. Don't just nod politely or scoff cynically. Chew on it until you understand the why and the how. Because we'll need that for the next bit.

THE DEPARTMENTS OF YES AND NO

The next bit is to start pushing feedback back up. It's where you as a boss take a hard look at what you're being asked to sign your team up for. And in December of 2020, you want to be taking a hard look. Your boss is asking your team for a commitment to an amount of work. So ask yourself some questions.

Is this work realistic? Is it sustainable? Is it healthy?

Some bosses are departments of yes. They always agree to the work because it's what the company needs, even if it puts their team at risk. Other bosses are departments of no. They see themselves as protectors of their team and default to pushing back in order to ensure their team has room to breathe.

Do you see yourself in either of these? Because neither of these are effective strategies.

A boss who consistently refuses to help is a boss who will get routed around or removed. A leader who burns out their team is putting massive risk on the books just to make their own boss like them. **To be good at this job, you need to get into the shit.** Why *this* target, and how much room is there to maneuver? If we had to trade X against Y, do we all agree that Y is more important? I can't commit the team to X unless we drop Y, Z, and anything else we're currently on the hook for.

People will not always like these answers, and that will be hard. But the thing we pay you for is to be the one who owns the health and effectiveness of your team. Maybe when you grapple with it and get into the details, the hard truth is that your team is too damaged by 2020 to be able to commit to much of anything in Q1. Then that's what we need you to say. And if the truth is that your team has been spared some of the brutality that others have faced and you have an ability to shoulder some extra load in Q1? Then we need you to say that, too. Speaking up with a thoughtful point of view that balances the needs of the team and the organization is leadership integrity. The world could do with more of that.

It's exactly that easy and it's exactly that hard. When goals flow top down in a deliberate way with a clear story, **that's alignment.** When every leader feeds back capacity and resilience information and the organization adapts, **that's predictability.** If we seem a bit extra on the subject of goals, this is why.

Everyone is telling you to rest. And of course you should rest. We are all worthy of, and deeply in need of, rest. But the bosses we know don't rest very well while their team is in chaos. And many times the people on their teams don't rest, either. Goals are hard work, we know. But they are how we buy ourselves some clarity. And for us, at least, clarity is what lets the rest actually happen.

· 22 ·

Has Your Eye Stopped Twitching Yet?

DECEMBER
30
2020

Many of you aren't working this week. And we're not either. Not really. We wondered if it made sense to write a newsletter about work and bossing when, for many of you, it will be one more thing in your inbox waiting for your return. If that's you and you're reading this in early Jan and stressing, please put us at the bottom of the pile. This email requires no reply.

And if you're reading us over break, we hope it's been restorative. That you've been able to step away. And been willing to let the out-of-office auto-responder carry the load for at least a little while.

On our end, we'd mostly lost track of what day it was. Oh, and you know that eye-flutter thing? The one where you've been staring at screens in low light and working from the couch for the better part of a year. At the end of 2020, everyone we knew was crash-landing into the holidays with a persistent eye flutter. Maybe you had one too?

Anyway, ours seem to be calming down. And if yours hasn't yet and you want the recipe, here's what we've got so far:

Step away from the computer. Take a break from squinting at a screen to make out the micro-changes in someone's expression and reconciling that against a laggy internet connection. And if you wear contacts, switch to glasses for a week.

TINY BUBBLES

In the moments when this year was utterly unbearable, one of us would say, "Well, at least we're in the same country." Depending on your perspective, that's either completely adorable or totally cringe. We get it.

But the thing people often miss about the two of us is that before we were married cofounders and co-parents, we were very long-distance—across several time zones and an international border. For years. When shit got rough, we'd always have this touchstone: Same country. Same city. Same house. Everything else, we'll figure out.

Do you remember that "deconstructed food" trend in the early '00s? The one where chefs would make essence of French toast and it would have maple foam on a brioche square and they'd call it Morning in Vermont?

That touchstone is deconstructed gratitude, stripped down to the core part that makes the rest of our lives possible.

There's all this research about how the happiest people have a regular gratitude practice.[1] For many folks, this can take the form of journaling or meditation. The shove is to shift your perspective—not to focus on all that is going wrong, but to start cataloging the things that are going right.

Our version starts with the core nugget, the place where if one thing had been different, everything would be different. It's a hell of a thing to hold the immenseness of it, but if you can do it, a bunch of other core nuggets start to appear.

SPEAKING OF GRATITUDE

Back in The Before, one of the things we would talk with people about was networking. It's clear that having an engaged network unlocks all sorts of opportunity, and not in a transactional way. The best networks build through mutual support and personal connection. We know this.

And we fucking hated networking.

It's hard to remember that right now. Honestly, if it were safe to have a big community get-together right now, we would pack a year's worth of hugs into the first hour. But the polite, small-talky sterility of most networking events left us exhausted. Every time. And we're pretty sure that feeling will come back, too.

The tool we gave people then was about how to activate your network without those awful events. And given that no one's hosting events right now anyhow, it feels like a good time to bring it back. It goes like this:

> Think about someone who helped you out. Maybe they stepped up in a massive way and they know it. Maybe it was a passing thing and they don't even remember, but you do. Think about someone who saw you. Who said the thing you needed to hear, or who opened a door, or closed one you shouldn't have gone through. Think about someone who got you through this year.

And now go say thank you. Say a specific thank-you that you've put some thought into. Don't have a follow-up ask. Don't expect them to reciprocate. Don't make this message do any work except to recognize the impact they had on you and let them sit in it. The icky parts of networking are where we're looking to exploit each other. So don't do that. Just put gratitude into the world.

One effect of this will be that that person is a more active part of your network now. They know that you recognize their effort, that it isn't wasted, and that you take it seriously. In most circumstances, network engagement matters more than network size. But a more important effect of this is that the world gets a little better. Our shattered sense of community heals a bit, all because you sent an email.

Thank you for 2020. Thank you for forwarding our stuff, and writing us to tell us when it hit. We're trying to make work better for people because we think it's possible and worthy and important. It makes us want to cry sometimes, to know that you get it and that you're still here with us working on it. Thank you for building this thing with us. Thank you for holding on. We'll see you in 2021.

· 23 ·

Who Tells You No?

JANUARY
13
2021

[On January 6, pro-Trump protesters stormed the U.S. Capitol building to interrupt certification of the electoral college results naming Joe Biden as the new U.S. president. Congresspeople and their staff were evacuated or barricaded in offices as protesters occupied the building for several hours. 5 people died, over 140 were injured, and in the days after the riot many social media sites started shutting down Donald Trump's accounts.]

If you want to be a thought leader, a great way to start is to furrow your brow, cross your arms, and make a distinction about "management vs leadership." It helps if it's pithy. *Management is doing things right and leadership is doing the right things.* That kind of thing.

When we start programs at RSG, one of the first things we do is dispense with all that. In most cases we use the terms interchangeably and mix in others like "boss" as well, because in practice the terms overlap almost completely.

You aren't an effective leader if you don't understand how to coordinate effort, communicate change, encourage constructive disagreement, and prioritize. You will be a mediocre manager (at best!) if you can't situate work within a broader context, motivate a team of individuals, and foster a shared sense of purpose.

Yes, there are purely managerial tasks. And yes, there are leaders with no management work to speak of. But in almost all real situations, good leaders understand management and good managers understand leadership. The overlaps matter more than the edges.

Except when they don't.

SO YOU'VE ABETTED AND BANKROLLED A COUP

Last week's shit in the U.S. was a mess. What else can you say? It was a mess, and the failures of leadership there are so bright they're impossible to ignore.

We may have more to say in this newsletter some time about the failures of elected leadership. Or the failures of military leadership. Or the failures of law enforcement leadership. There are certainly things to be said. But there are the failures of tech leadership, too. And those are the ones in our own backyard.

In the aftermath of January 6, Facebook, Twitter, YouTube, Shopify, and a handful of others de-platformed the President of the United States. At least a little bit. And some folks wanted to talk about what a show of *leadership* that was.

We don't pretend that it's easy, kicking off a sitting U.S. president. We suspect that a lot of very senior, very loud government officials were calling these companies to demand reversals. That was probably hard.

But... Any account of the leadership showed by these companies on January 6 needs to include the leadership they failed to show leading up to it, too. Facebook and Twitter shut down Trump the day after the attacks. But Facebook and Twitter are where those attacks were planned—out loud, in the open.

YouTube took down some videos after conspiracy theorists stormed the capitol. But YouTube is where those conspiracy theories were hatched. Shopify took down Trump's merch store. But Shopify is the economic engine for every hate group clever enough to keep the N-word off their mugs. At time of writing you can still buy "Black Lives MAGA" T-shirts and actual fucking Hitler Youth knives from Shopify stores. And the company still takes a cut of the purchase price every time someone checks out... despite their *leadership.*

How did we get here? These leaders can see why violent and hateful rhetoric is a bad thing, right? That's why they made the decisions they did on January 7? So then why didn't they make them months, or years ago?[1]

THE HIGHER THE FEWER

We have this idea that the hard decisions get easier the higher you go in an organization. That by the time you're a VP, nobody can tell you shit. If a call is the wrong call, you've got everything you need to speak up in the moment.

For some VPs, that's true. But for many folks, the same dynamic that kept them from speaking up as an intern is still playing out years later. Concern about sounding stupid. About getting labeled as negative or problematic by their colleagues. The feeling that their seat at the table is precarious in the first place.

The worry that your job is on the line if you say the wrong thing doesn't go away when your salary increases. If anything, the stakes are higher. The people making those decisions are peers now, not far-off executives. There's a sense that you're supposed to toe the line publicly. And sometimes, lazily, you end up doing that privately, too. You shut up and nod along. We know this because we've done this.

We meet so many bosses who lament that their organization is moving in a direction they don't support. Our first questions are always the same: "Do they know? Have you said those words out loud?"

Most of the time, the answer is "no." No, I don't agree with a set of decisions happening within my organization. And no, I haven't spoken up. 🙁

"NO" IS IMPORTANT FEEDBACK

We teach leaders how to give effective feedback to their own people, and at the end of every session, someone raises the money question.

"Hey, so, how do I get my people to give me feedback?"

We love this question. This is a leader grappling with their own power. And tucked underneath this question are at least 63 other questions. How do I honor that power differential? Why would someone tell me their honest opinion when they know they might get fired? How do I, as a leader, create space for people to tell me to fuck off if they think we're heading down the wrong path? And do I even want that?

A lot of leaders don't want that. But most of the folks we talk to do. In particular, we hear this from CEOs. They want a senior team that challenges them and makes them better. They are paying executive salaries. They want executives in those seats, not bobbleheads nodding yes all day. But that's what they've got.

What gives?

THE WORST BRAND IN ORGANIZATIONAL DEVELOPMENT

Psychological safety couldn't have a worse name. We've talked about the concept here before,[2] but we always start with a disclaimer: Psychological safety isn't about a workplace full of snowflakes who are too sensitive to get real feedback. It's not about coddling your people. And it's expressly not about avoiding hard conversations.

Psychological safety is the opposite of that. It's "I know what's expected of me." The systems of evaluation are clear—I get what's in bounds and out of bounds, both in regards to the work and around how the work gets done. It takes the implicit elements of work and makes them explicit. And because I have that clarity, I'm able to take chances. My creative energy goes toward the work itself not guessing whether I'll get fired for disagreeing.

The short answer for those CEOs is that no one will tell you no unless they're safe to do so. They see risks in your business. They have information you need. But if you don't create an environment where it's safe for them to bring that to you, they won't. If bobblehead leadership is what's rewarded in your org, that's what you'll get.

We're seeing this play out all over the news right now: leaders, surrounded by people who tell them what they want to hear, reacting, flatfooted, to things that were obvious the whole way along to anyone paying attention. Obvious, we should note, to their staff, too—a sea of people who could have told them no, and made them better, more proactive leaders...if they felt like they could.

And if, as a leader, this is getting you curious about how to cultivate psychological safety—if you want tools for building diverse teams of engaged, active participants who push you and themselves—well...That's management. And it's a toolset every leader needs.

· 24 ·

If There's Light at the End of the Tunnel, Why Is It Still So Dark?

JANUARY
27
2021

In five weeks it will be March again.

That's a hell of a thing, isn't it? If you're an Aries or later, you're coming up on your second pandemic birthday. It's been almost a year of this.

Back in March, we were all reading about grief.[1] Remember that article? It talked about how we were doing a strange, anticipatory grief back then—grieving the losses we hadn't felt yet, but could see coming. Well... They came.

We're all figuring it out, of course. None of us is new to this anymore.[2] We have a system for groceries, weekly Zoom calls. We have found ways to endure and find the moments of joy in the midst of it all.

But in the last few weeks it's striking how many people just. Feel. Flat. It's like all the deferrals, and "soon, I hopes" and "can't wait untils" have claimed their energy. Parked it, in some future post-COVID place. Again, it's not that there's no joy—humans always find ways to create moments of joy. But a lot of them seem to be finding it harder to access at the moment.[3]

ONE FOOT IN FRONT OF THE OTHER

We're back in lockdown in Toronto. Though, honestly, in so many ways it feels like we never left. We're back to waving at neighbors who are often the only in-person interaction we have all week.

"How are you?" they holler from the end of the driveway.

"Okay," we holler back. "You?"

"Holding up. It's hard."

We've been reading more history books. In particular, ones where people live through grand upheaval—though, to be fair, this is most history books. We tell our kids that their grandkids won't believe it. Someday it will be unimaginable.

For now, we take it one day at a time. And if that sounds cliché, it's because it is. It is the cliché of the moment, the cliché people pull out of their pocket dictionary of clichés for times like these. It's right next to "This too shall pass" in the *How to Muscle through Untenable Shit* section.

Back when we were in the fog,[4] we talked about small movements, about how in fog, you slow way down because you can't see the way forward. That's not where we are anymore. We can see more clearly. We can guess pretty well what the next few months will feel like, and even feel hopeful about the months after that. But for a lot of us, when we try to hold it all in our heads, our brains refuse. Everyone is reaching the point of being overwhelmed much faster than usual. We're hearing from more folks that they start at the top of their to-do lists and read them all the way to the bottom only to start at the top again without getting anything done. Eventually, through sheer force of will, they pick one. A small one.

Moving one foot. And then another. And tomorrow they wake up and do it all again. One day at a time.

Maybe this is you and maybe it isn't. But if you're leading a team, understand that many of your people are doing this. And if so, here are some things you can do to help.

PRIORITIZATION VS. INERTIA

For folks who are struggling to get started, there are two common culprits: prioritization and inertia. The symptoms looks similar, but the treatments are different.

If people on your team are struggling to get themselves rolling, a good place to start is to ask them, "Is this a problem of too many, or too big?" Truthfully, they will probably answer, "Too many AND too big oh my god." Fair enough. It may be that your team needs help with prioritization *and* inertia these days. But most bosses we work with find that it helps to have a system for thinking it through.

When prioritization is the issue, I stare at the to-do list. I don't know where to start because everything seems important. I need a clearer idea of what matters most, how it connects to what the organization as a whole is trying to get done. And I may need permission for some thing(s) to be dropped in service of that higher-priority stuff.

To help, I need a boss to say, "If you can do only one thing, make it this."

When inertia is the issue, I can't get started because I am at a standstill. Objects at rest stay at rest, and I can't access the energy to start myself up again. The instinct to make the work smaller and then smaller again? It doesn't do a damn thing to solve for prioritization, but it reduces the amount of energy I need to get rolling. And once I am moving, it's easier to keep going.

To help, bosses can break the work into smaller pieces. Bosses are well positioned here. We often came up through the work our teams are now doing. And even if you didn't, you can still be a sounding board. Ask your people how they might break down complex tasks into discrete steps. One foot in front of the other. One day at a time.

WE ALL NEED THINGS TO LOOK FORWARD TO

Another benefit of chunking work into smaller bits is that you have more moments to celebrate. And right now, we could all use some tiny wins.

We don't need bosses to pretend a small win is a huge win. Do not coddle or patronize your teams. They will see through it, we promise. But as we enter year two of a global pandemic, even our small wins are remarkable. And they are worthy of celebration—even if the celebration is commensurate with the size of the win.

We also desperately need things to look forward to. And the obvious pick—the idea of things going back to normal—is too big to hold in our heads. It's an avatar for our grief, for everything we've deferred, and it amplifies every restriction that is still in place. There *is* a light at the end of this long, dark tunnel, but it is still many small steps away, and their enumeration is what feels so overwhelming.

So yes, look forward to a vaccine or herd immunity or hugging your people. But we are growing impatient. We need shorter timelines. We need to look forward to things and then for those things to *happen*.

In our house, this past week, it was French fries. Really good French fries, from a place that got takeout right. We swear those French fries made us want to cry. It'd been almost a year since we'd had proper fries. Your version doesn't have to be twice-fried potatoes, but it can be that small or silly or frivolous. And it doesn't have to make sense to anyone but you. But you absolutely need good, reachable things to look forward to because hope has its own inertia. When you feel like you're stuck, you need something to kickstart it again. Go small to get going.

One foot. Then the other. We got this.

· 25 ·

Hovering Over Decline and Clicking Accept

FEBRUARY
10
2021

Ours is a house that cooks ahead. Anytime we're making food, we're making more than is strictly necessary. Rice going in the rice cooker? May as well put in whatever will fit. Just did a big order from the greengrocer? How many veggies can you put in a curry before you're breaking some sort of international law?

Leftovers are often unloved. There's an old joke about a preacher saying grace over a plate of leftovers and finishing with "It seems to me that I have blessed a good deal of this material before."

But you could do worse than a life with lots of leftovers. On the plus side, most of the work is already done by the time you go to reheat it. You also avoid the thing where 40% of food in North American houses goes in the garbage.[1]

But whether you like to cook or not, this is for you. We hope it helps.

WE TIRED

There's a tech reporter at the *New York Times* who was tweeting earlier this week.[2] She's got a book coming out. And small children. And did we mention a day job at he *Times*? And it's the middle of a fucking pandemic.

She said mom friends were asking how she did it all. Was she superhuman? And her response was, "Nope, I just cried a lot and neglected other things in my life."

This is all of us right now.

But the specific thing that she's describing—*modulo* the pandemic part—is deeply familiar around here.

When we started Raw Signal Group, our youngest was a little over a year old. She didn't sleep for the first eight months of life. We were running on fumes before we even made our way to the starting line. We were writing *HFUIYM*,[3] trying to get a new business off the ground, and still not sleeping a whole lot.

When you're exhausted, a lot of your poor decision making ends up making things worse. And so the first step in getting out of this awful spot is a loose approximation of the Hippocratic oath.

First, stop shooting yourself in the foot.

This can be hard to see when you're in the thick of it. Most of your instincts are upside down, and what feels like a shortcut or a quick win often comes back to bite you later. One of the most powerful things you can do from this place of being overwhelmed is to bring back that visibility, to be able to see what's causing harm... and what's helping.

BORROWING FROM FUTURE YOU

When shit gets rocky, a normal and healthy instinct is to borrow from your future self. Most of us learn early to prioritize aggressively during a crisis, and that means a lot of things get punted. "Quick syncs" get rescheduled two weeks out, alongside dental cleanings and oil changes.

You know you'll still have to do those things, but it's Future You's problem. You block up some of Future You's calendar because Present You needs that time back. And, in a normal crisis, things do lighten up after the shock. And then Future You pays off the debts that Past You accumulated. And you get your buffer back and your shoulders come down and you can breathe again.

But these 11 months haven't been a normal crisis. They've been a chronic, rolling chain of crisis after crisis,[4] like one of those mile-long trains trundling through a rail crossing. Delaying everything. Ringing alarm bells and flashing lights but not in any particular rush. With no end in sight except the intellectual knowledge that it can't go on forever. And all the while brutally violent if you try to cross it.

And what we've seen is that a lot of people are still borrowing from their future selves. They're going deeper into debt. More deferrals. More rescheduling. Calendars that are a solid wall of obligations weeks ahead of time and new, time-sensitive stuff still trying to force itself in, into the 15 minutes you hoped would be lunch. Or before the first thing. Or after the last thing.[5]

It's hard to blame Past You. Past You was trying to get through their own mess from the month before, and the month before that. But if you're someone staring down this debt right now, you know that you've run out of room. Present You needs to start working differently or else Future You is... fucked.

INVESTING IN FUTURE YOU

If we're honest, this week is probably already fucked.

The most unhelpful piece of advice for most people during a pandemic is *"Take some time today for self-care."* Like, if that's advice you can take today, by all means please do. We're serious. If you have room in your calendar and an ability to nurture your own health, you should seize that moment. It's precious and important and valid for you to do that.

Many of you don't have the ability to take that advice, though, because today was already decided days, if not weeks, ago. Past You put some debt on your books that you're paying off today. So be it.

But... For most of you there is some future week right now that is not yet a mess. It might be next week, or it might be out in March, but there's a week that hasn't piled up with stuff yet because that stuff hasn't had a chance to happen. Future You is going to live that week. And you have an opportunity to set it up.

The truth about most calendar-run organizations is that calendars are law. If it's on the calendar, it's real. And if it's empty, it's up for grabs. In an ideal world, you would have empty swaths on your calendar where you could breathe. But in reality, the minute someone sees an empty slot, they claim it, and you're right back to the wall-to-wall meetings you've been trying to get out from under for the better part of a year.

HACKING YOUR CALENDAR TO PROTECT YOURSELF

First: Book time with yourself. Many of you already do this, but for those who don't, it's a bloody revelation. The calendar is law, and if you book a 30-minute recurring meeting with yourself to eat some lunch, that becomes truth. Like putting a rock into a river—everything else just flows around it. It helps to mark this meeting private. If yours is not a culture where private meetings will fly, give it a name people's eyes bounce off of. "Goals check in." Or "Quick sync." Invite a colleague who needs the same calendar defense. Calendrical mutual aid is always legitimate, but especially in a crisis.

Second: There are things on your calendar that have to happen but that don't care when they happen—meetings that wouldn't be okay to cancel but would be fine to reschedule the same day. This is important because the calendar doesn't care what time things happen, but you do. You have different energy at 10 a.m. or 3 p.m. or 8 p.m. There isn't a right or wrong there—chronotypes are a real thing.[6] Learning this about yourself and arranging your day to do the right work at the right time is an executive superpower.

If you don't know this about yourself yet, go look at January's calendar. Which parts of the day felt great, and which ones felt awful? (You may need to grade on a curve here.) You'll likely figure out that 10 a.m. is a great time for writing but that a bad meeting at that time derails your day. Or you'll figure out that *you* are the bad meeting that other people have at 10 a.m. and need to reshuffle to protect them from your nonsense. Whatever it is, we are in harm reduction mode here, and these are gifts to Future You that start paying down debt instead of continuing to spend it.

There's so much written about self-care, and much of it starts from a good place but falls apart the moment things get hectic. But this idea of Past You working in service of Future You isn't a one-off. It's not a massage you sneak in one Friday morning, the secret hope that 60 minutes of hot rocks will counteract 12 hours a day hunched over a laptop.

This is an ongoing daily practice. And through this lens, leftovers are beautiful. They are nourishment that your past self gifted to your future self. Because you knew what you were staring down this week. And that a repetitive lunch was better than a hangry Future You.

· 26 ·

The Beginning of the End

FEBRUARY
24
2021

The pandemic isn't over just because you're over it.

Those of you on TikTok just hummed that line.[1] Back in early pandemic, Heather Chelan's upbeat track was everywhere, featured in an array of videos highlighting non-pandemic-safe activities.

That was back when we were still outraged that politicians went on vacation while telling us to stay home.[2] Or that a salesman kept traveling even after he'd lost his sense of smell and taste.[3] When we were still trying to get Boomer parents to follow the rules and they refused to comply, like overgrown teenagers.

That seems like a long time ago—not only the outrage but the idea that we would all be in it together.

We've been at this a year, and the longer we're at it, the less together it feels.

TOO TIRED FOR OUTRAGE

As we approach the anniversary of the first lockdowns, we're not over the pandemic per se, but we are very over the outrage.

The anger and frustration at people not adhering to public health guidelines? Replaced by a shrug.

What can you do? People are going to make poor decisions. Eleven months in, it's not my job to remind you that the mask doesn't work if it's not affixed over your nose.

How do you not know that by now? And if you know it, how do you not care?

More profound than the shrug is the underlying fatigue—the sheer exhaustion of a year spent laying bare the truth as it has always been. We are all in it together... except some of us aren't in it at all.

We're not trying to be downers, but there is a real thing happening and we should talk about it, because the shrug is important, and there's an awful lot that's coming along with it.

If the outrage was at one end of the pendulum, apathy is at the other. And when it swung, it swung hard.

Outrage is a response to the interconnectedness of everything. It also gets at a core piece of the human experience: this idea of fairness. If you're doing the work to stem the spread of COVID but no one else is, that work is futile. It also means there's a set of glaring inequalities about your life in relationship to others.

Those people get to travel. They get to see grandparents. They go grocery shopping at a leisurely pace. They get to catch up with friends. And you... don't.

Humans are incredibly sensitive to fairness. A natural first response to things being unfair is rage. But a year of rage and there's not much left in the tank. What's left is a deep ache—the hurt of having to stop doing these things and the hurt of watching others keep right on doing them. And faced with ongoing reminders of unfairness, a bunch of us have retreated inward.

THE SHRUG AT WORK

It's not just that this shrug is happening with neighbors and friends. It's happening with random strangers. And it's also playing out across our workplaces.

Right now, many of us are having a hard time tracking anything more than what's in front of us. We're living a tiny little serenity prayer and spending all our effort on the things that we can control.

At work, lots of folks are finding it hard to track externalities. And even if they can, who has the energy to go chasing them? As though we need any more reminders that other people's poor decisions can adversely impact us! It's no wonder that that move inward is showing up at work, too.

People are onboarding into teams where they still haven't met most of their colleagues. We have bosses so stacked in meetings that they can only on focus what their team is meant to deliver. And while they have a small island of work happening, there's limited communication with the rest of the org.

We're setting our goals in literal and figurative isolation. And if you feel like fiefdoms have been popping up at work, that's because they have been. We ask leaders about their company culture and they ask us, "You mean before? Or now?"

And the reason they need to clarify is because the "before" answer is radically different. It's not that they don't have culture now; it's just that the answer is team specific not org-wide because many of them have never experienced what it's like when the whole company is together. They have no notion of org-wide culture because they joined in a **post-org-wide-culture era.** And yes, if you're a boss, you should go reread that sentence and let that sink all the way in.

PRODUCTIVITY HAS NEVER BEEN HIGHER

Okay, so we're all more isolated but like, so what? Right? Keeping yourself safe is a good thing. Withdrawing from spaces and relationships that are overwhelming or harmful is a healthy choice. Honestly, it's one we wish we'd both learned sooner.

But when everything is a source of anxiety, when you're so fried that you withdraw from *every* relationship and *every* space, when your day becomes pull inward, keep your head down, keep yourself hydrated, and do what you can to get through it... When that happens, we should talk about what we lose.

The answer is not productivity. There are a plenty of CEOs out there who still want to talk about how productivity hasn't dropped. Well, sure. We've seen layoffs, office closures, and a semipermanent two-hour expansion of the workday. Per-employee productivity is through the roof right now.

But it doesn't feel good, because we have lost other, more important things.

We don't want to care anymore about our neighbors' social distancing. *But we do care about our neighbors.* We don't want to care about some other team's priorities and decisions. *But we do care about our colleagues,* about doing good work together. And the withdrawing, meant to protect us, ends up doing its own damage.

Isolating ourselves also means isolating others, because another thing that suffers when everyone in a workplace (or a society) pulls inward is allyship. The scarcity creeps in—of time; of attention; of energy to reply to a message asking the group for help, not knowing where those reserves are going to come from. Of willingness to go to bat *yet again* to make sure the right people are even included on the fucking meeting invite.

It's fair to need rest. To have moments when you know you're no good to nobody. But what happens when we all withdraw at the exact same time?

A SPRAINED METAPHOR

If you've ever sprained something, or torn something, or gone through a round of physiotherapy, you know this: After an injury, the damaged muscle tightens up to protect itself, to prevent things from getting worse. Which is great—until it isn't. Because once the threat is gone, the injured muscle is still tight, sometimes so tight that it hurts to move. So tight that all you can do is shrug.

The only way to get your range of motion back is through slow, intentional, careful stretching. It starts when you notice that you're hunched over. Some of you just sat up straighter in your chair. You can laugh about it if you want, but it's a good start. The reconnecting is important. Take a deep breath while you're at it.

We can't tell you what kind of stretch you need. It might be about connecting with people on your team who you've never met outside of a Zoom window, or replying to the email asking for help that you keep marking as unread. Whatever it is, it's gonna feel awkward to extend again, to reintegrate with stuff you'd shut out. Physio folks say, "Discomfort is okay; pain means we stop for a bit."

In three weeks it will be spring. Again. The experts (and the TikTokers) say that the pandemic isn't over and we've still got a long way to go. But we might be at the beginning of the end. As we step back into the sunlight, we've all got some healing to do. But a thing that's clear—that's obvious once we say it—is that none of us can do it alone.

· 27 ·

Can You Talk About Why Everyone Is Quitting?

MARCH
10
2021

We've gotten this question three times in the last week. To be fair, we've been talking about pandemic quitting for a while now.

We mentioned the idea of a "huge reshuffling of talent" back in May,[1] and talked about people wanting to reclaim space between work and life in June.[2] We talked about it again in July[3] and about how to know if the situation was fixable. Hell, we even wrote an entire how to quit in a pandemic guide in September.[4]

That we're at the one-year mark for the first lockdowns and it feels like everyone is quitting, well, we can't say we're surprised. But it's our full-time job to pay attention to this stuff. And what we're hearing from a lot of you is: Why now?

BUT WHY, ACTUALLY, NOW?

We're starting to stare down coming back. And the thing that's clear to most folks is that they *can't* go back. The person they were at the start of this is long gone.

And you know it for your own self if you've gotten those "One Year Ago" photo app reminders this week. The person in those pictures has no idea what's about to happen. How could they?

For many of us, that former self is unrecognizable. So beautiful. So hopeful. And so, so naive.

We'll have the kids home for two weeks, and then they'll go back. Might be sorta nice to have an extended spring break anyway.

We're not new anymore. We're not naive. We're not those people. And the idea of going back to a workforce that anticipates an outdated version of us makes it easier to think about what's next.

DON'T CALL IT A COMEBACK

As we anticipate our collective reentry, it's easy to understand the appeal of a fresh start. The opportunity for new coworkers, ones who haven't seen us take a shower on Zoom[5] or wipe our kid's bum or apply a face mask only to find it was a video-on call instead of audio only.

We're ready to reclaim more of that space. On the heels of a year of this, the entire workforce is screaming GET THE FUCK OUT OF MY HOUSE. Get out of my evenings. Get out of my weekends. Get out of my before-sleep brain loops. And my morning coffees. And my Peleton rides spent listening to webinars.

The collective pushback against employers who have been in our living rooms, our bedrooms, our kitchens, and our family life for the better part of a year... it's not a gentle shove.

SOME SLATES DON'T WIPE CLEAN

In our office it was always the red whiteboard marker. Green, blue, purple, orange would all wipe clean off on the first try. But once you'd written on the whiteboard with the red one, it was on there forever.

If you've ever lived this life, you know the trick. The best way to clear a whiteboard marker that won't come off is to write over top of it with another marker. The solvent content in the new marker helps lift the old one. You have to write new things to make the old things fade... So when we see that a lot of people are starting new jobs right now, we get it.

But where does that leave your organization? And what's your job as a boss in this moment?

Well, first let's recognize where we are. A year of pandemic has written a lot on each of us, and much of it is in permanent marker. For your employees who have been with you through the whole thing, there's no getting around it. COVID is part of your employer brand for those people. Always will be.

Even for those who started with your organization part-way through the pandemic, this is part of their story, part of how they talk about their work, part of how they think about their future with—or without—you.

As a boss, now is a good time to listen. You know the listening that happens when you step out of the car and into a forest and it takes a second for your ears to open up? Compared to the noise of the car, the forest seems so silent. But no forest is ever actually silent. It's just that sometimes it takes a deliberate effort to notice how much you'd turned down the volume on everything.

Listen to what your workforce is trying to tell you. Because from over here where we're writing this, they're speaking loudly. They are burnt crispy. They are tired. They are working too much and living too little. They need to reestablish boundaries. They want a clean start and a life healthier than how it's felt. And the idea of that is *so attractive* that, one way or another, they're going to get it.

WE'RE HAVING ANOTHER MOMENT

Quitting is one way for your people to set new boundaries and negotiate a new relationship with work. As a boss, your next job is to ask yourself: Are there any others? Is that renegotiation something they can do within your org? And if so, what does that look like?

Back in the spring, we told you that every organization had a moment in front of them[6]—a moment to decide what kind of pandemic employer they were going to be. Everything was on the table. And organizations made some wildly different choices—choices they are still living with, a year on.

This is a moment again. And this time the question is how you want to meet your team as they come out of all this. How are you going to give back the hours of lengthened workday? How will you support them as they try to reset some work/life boundaries?

It's gotta be you who starts this conversation, because you hold the power to make change. We should all want to build supportive workplaces where employees feel empowered, sure. But a lot of people aren't feeling very empowered right now. A lot of employees feel like the only power they have left is the power to walk away. And when they use that power, even with all the risk and uncertainty it creates for them, there's a reason.

So our advice to you is to get proactive about this negotiation. Don't make this as-needed or when-requested. This is a conversation worth having with every single person on your team. What's working? What's not? What needs to change as we emerge from lockdown?

Imagine that every person on your team is trying to figure out whether this job is recoverable or not. Imagine that it's been a hard year but that many of them are still open to the idea of staying on. Imagine that they're curious to see what you're going to do next but that they aren't going to wait much longer.

· 28 ·

Elijah, You Need to Unmute

MARCH
24
2021

"Do you want us to dial you in for seder?"

It's Passover this week, and our family in the States is all getting together. In person. Mask free. Post-vaccination. To dip twice. To eat matzo-ball soup. To sing an Aramaic song about a goat. You know, the usual.

The seder they've designed has a lot in common with the one from 2019. They'll open all the windows (just to be safe), but otherwise, it's almost indistinguishable. Except...

Except that the Canadian cousins aren't there. We're still on the other side of a closed border. We still haven't had shots. And we're still waiting to see how the next little bit shakes out.

And so the question facing us this week is the question facing a lot of folks right now:

What do we do when some people are able to gather again, but not everyone? Do we do it fully in person but know that some folks won't be able to join? Do we go fully remote again and relive the seder of 2020? The one where no one could hear because our relatives had not yet mastered the unmute button. The one where no one could hug because Zoom instances are a poor proxy for in-person gathering.

Fully remote, fully in person, or a mix of the two. This is the question that will dominate the rest of this year and into the next. The extremes are the easiest to navigate.

If it's in person only, either you figure out how to get there or you don't. Either you're vaccinated or you're not. You move back to the city to come into the office every day. Or you don't. You travel for the big conference or you stay home.[1] It's not inclusive, but it's clear.

In the remote-only version, everyone is welcome to have the same subpar experience. We're all invited to stumble over the same technology, stretched to its limits. We get the shittier version, but it's inclusive. You can join if you're unwell, unvaccinated, home with kids, far from transit, or unable to cross a border.

The mix of the two, well, that's where it gets messy.

HYBRID ORGS ARE DOOMED

We came up in internet-enabled hybrid work 1.0.

At Mozilla, we'd hire folks wherever they were in the world, and that's on top of inviting in a global open-source community. The sun never set on the Firefox empire.

Before Zoom was a glimmer in its founders' eyes, every Mozilla meeting had remote participants. Every office had multicamera video rigs and boom mics in the ceilings. We beta-tested Skype-driven telepresence robots that would roam the halls in Mountain View[2]... until someone inevitably drove them into an elevator and they lost Wi-Fi.

The technology we have today is so much better, and so much more evenly distributed, than it was back then. But outside of robots stuck in elevators, technology is never the problem. The problem is deeper.

Here's how it went down back then.

The people in California work at headquarters. Most, but not all, of the people they work with are in the same office. They have a question, they walk over to a colleague and ask it. They own the calendar invites for a lot of the organization's meetings. All of those meetings default to PST business hours.

The Californians also have a lot of hallway discussions. Those discussions build ambient awareness—not only about what other folks are working on, but also the general direction of the business. That ambient awareness helps the Californians get promoted, disproportionately. Those promotions further concentrate power within HQ. Remote employees complain that they have fewer opportunities for advancement. They aren't wrong.

Some of the Californians start managing people in Germany. Working with no overlapping daylight hours means a bunch of lag on simple questions. The Berliner has a question at 9 a.m. their time and has to wait until 5 p.m. their time for the boss to wake up on the West Coast. This leads to a bunch of sleeplessness for the Californian and a bunch of resentment for the Berliner.

And even when you're not trying to hybrid-org across the globe, there are still major issues. Like forgetting to put a Zoom link in the calendar invite. Forgetting to capture the hallway conversation so someone who isn't in the office knows that the feature's been killed. Forgetting to order the laptop for the new hire who is onboarding remotely. Forgetting to onboard that person at all.

None of these problems are about malice. And they aren't about the tech stack, either.

The biggest impediment to the future of work is how easy it is to remember the people close to you and how easy it is to forget those farther away. And these are problems that stem from a lack of care.

Humans can *function* in a lot of different contexts, but it takes care to help them *thrive.* It takes thoughtful, deliberate design to ensure that your people—*all* your people—feel heard, included, and supported.

Offices aren't great at this, to be clear. Modern open-plan offices in particular have a set of norms that can work directly against these things. But if you plow ahead into remote or hybrid setups without thinking it through, you can do so much worse.

HYBRID ORGS ARE THE FUTURE

On the one hand, we have this once-in-a-generation opportunity to invent a different way to work. We get to decide which things we take from the last year, and the years before that, and which things we leave behind. And on the other, we know that there's the potential to do a lot of harm. The good version of hybrid organization is inclusive and dynamic and individual. The bad version is ambiguous and gaslighting.

So let's talk about how to know which one you're building.

It starts with showing your work. The best predictor of where your culture will be in two years is the care you put in today. Not the pithy Future of Work quotes that CEOs give to the press. What's the careful, deeply thought through version? And how clear is it to everyone?

Can your remote staff really be anywhere? *Anywhere?* Do you have expectations around time zones? Will you tie compensation to my location? What if my location changes? Can I move around? Can I move to a jurisdiction with different labor laws? Some countries have *very exciting* labor laws, so this is worth getting right.

And how about inclusion? If we leave in-person/remote up to individual choice, will it suck to make a different choice? If I am a remote-only employee on a team of choose-to-be-in-the-office colleagues, do I have a second-class experience? Am I choosing that with eyes open, or is my company telling me that I am an equal employee but giving me unequal opportunity?

What's our plan for communication and coordination of effort? If it's "Slack and Jira and Zoom," do we have a plan for everyone hating that idea? What structural supports are we going to build to bring every employee into the future of work? Or, failing that, how are we going to tell the employees we're leaving behind?

This list isn't exhaustive, even if it's exhausting. There are great, fair, honest answers to all of these questions, answers that are true to the company you work in. That are clear and inclusive and full of care. Answers that can withstand sunlight.

There's such an aching, powerful need for work to change right now. Your organization can be part of that. *You* can be part of that. But it will take new, thoughtful answers to these questions, or else inertia will have us filling in the old answers again. The same work done the same way...except maybe with the windows open.

EPILOGUE

It’s Not Worth It

MAY
19
2021

The sun is out. Yesterday, we ran three whole blocks to catch an ice cream truck. The music, bouncing through the neighbourhood, pulled every child within a square mile out of their homes.

We're teaching our youngest about commerce. She wants to know how much things cost and which coins are worth what. And she points to every face and asks if that, too, is Queen Elizabeth. Most of the time, the answer is yes.

We stare at the price list and figure out that she has enough for a small cone with sprinkles. And a coin left over to say "thank you so much"—which is how she understands tipping.

We have to explain it all like she's five, because she is.

Count up what you've got. Look at what's on offer. Figure out what happens next. It's happening everywhere we look right now. And many people doing that math are deciding it's not worth it.

- Complaints that no one wants to go to work[1] in a low-wage, low-job-security, low-benefits position. Countered by employers seeing hundreds of applicants for living-wage jobs in the same industry.

- Media CEOs demanding that journalists come back to the office. Communicated in an 800-word op-ed worth of "because I said so." Followed by the newsroom blacking out the publication.[2]

- And tech companies saying, "We care about politics when it helps us hire you. But after that please don't mention it again kthx." And then watching a third of their team walk out the door because that level of bullshit is not worth it.[3]

We said it at the start of all this[4]—that by the time we came back, we'd be different, even if the jobs and the offices we left were the same. We'd have changed on a deep level, transformed beyond recognition.

Early on, CEOs talked about doing a decade of digital transformation in a fortnight. Well, it wasn't just the machines. Whatever timetables the Future of Work people had, they didn't consider the past year. Promise.

After a year of us being burnt out, crispy fried, work from home but mostly living at work, employers are asking if we're ready to come back. Back to commutes and shitty coffee and incompetent management (working on that last one as fast as we can). And for a lot of folks, when they stare down the list, the answer is clear.

It's not worth it.

It's not worth it to sit in a gas line, to sit in traffic, to sit at a desk, to sit in traffic, to sit in another gas line.

It's not worth it to keep playing when the game is clearly rigged, when Grade 5 probability coursework can predict who you're gonna promote.

On the heels of finding fullness and meaning in less than 1000 square feet, we are so clear on what matters and what does not. Which things on the list we care about and which ones aren't for us anymore, even if they once were.

What would be worth it?

Bosses, listen: Most people want to do a good job at work. People are pragmatic. They are flexible, they are forgiving, and they will give a lot of grace to an organization that gets the basics right. A lot of your job as a leader in an organization is to not fuck things up so badly that you run out that grace.

The work. Give us a reasonable workload and the tools to do it. *Tell* us what's expected, instead of having us guess, and ground those expectations in reality. Your people are not bothered by accountability or by working hard. Many of them take pride in doing a great job. What bothers people is burn-out workloads, shifting goalposts, and an unending need for heroics to make up for bad planning.

And when we do that great job, make sure we're recognized for it. People want very different things when it comes to recognition, so this is a place you'll have to talk with each of us. Some want applause at an all-hands, and for others that will make them want to disappear into their chair. But every employee you have wants to be paid and promoted fairly—fairly relative to their peers, fairly relative to their industry and expertise, and fairly relative to what it costs to live their lives. If your business can't pay people fairly, it's a bad business.[5]

The team. We can collaborate as a diverse array of colleagues and do great work for your organization. Just please stop hiring unapologetically hateful people. Nothing saps the morale of an otherwise high-performing team like being asked to re-defend their right to be here.[6]

That is not an ideological purity test; that is bare minimum psychological safety. You can give people room to have grown and made amends, but treat those claims with every bit of the healthy curiosity you'd apply to any other claim on their résumé. Take accountability for the safety of your employees. Fix the missing stair.[7]

The company. We live in a community—several communities, really—and we're done with companies who pretend that they dont. We understand—we genuinely do understand—that it's hard to thread the needle on social issues. That it's hard to "keep everyone happy." But we need you to understand that when you tell us to "keep it outside of work channels," you're failing us. You're giving a simplistic answer to a complex problem.

Some people's lives are politicized, whether they want them to be or not. And to navigate that, even at work, those people may need to talk about it. To tell their story. To find allies. To feel that they are seen and belong and that the needs of their community are ones that their employer cares about. A more complete answer will require making some uncomfortable decisions about where your organization stands, instead of just pretending that it doesn't need to make those decisions.

The rest. For the rest, for our life outside of work, just leave it alone. Be clear about when we can be offline, and don't secretly hold it against us when we take your word. Explicitly allocate the most generous vacation you can stomach. Then figure out why your people don't feel safe taking it, and fix that.

Or don't.

You can ignore everything we've written here, and most days your company won't burst into flames. For the most part you probably won't even break any laws. You'll just have a shittier business and maybe a shittier life. That's all.

Your best people, full of passion and ready to bring their all to the work you do, are standing there in front of the ice cream truck. They know what they bring to the table. They are looking at what you're offering. Salary, benefits, perks. Sprinkles. All that. But also the work, the team, the company, and the rest. And they're trying to decide if it's worth it.

Notes

1 OUR JOB NOW IS TO FLATTEN THE CURVE

1. Lydia Ramsey Pflanzer, "One slide in a leaked presentation for US hospitals reveals that they're preparing for millions of hospitalizations as the outbreak unfolds," *Business Insider*, 6 Mar. 2020, www.businessinsider.com/presentation-us-hospitals-preparing-for-millions-of-hospitalizations-2020-3.
2. Silvia Stringhini, "1/ I may be repeating myself" [thread], Twitter, 9 Mar. 2020, twitter.com/silviast9/status/1236933818654896129.
3. Matias Grez, "Jurgen Klopp incredulous at coronavirus question following defeat by Chelsea," CNN Sports, 5 Mar. 2020, edition.cnn.com/2020/03/04/football/liverpool-chelsea-fa-cup-jurgen-klopp-spt-intl.
4. Siouxsie Wiles, "The three phases of Covid-19—and how we can make it manageable," *The Spinoff*, 9 Mar. 2020, thespinoff.co.nz/society/09-03-2020/the-three-phases-of-covid-19-and-how-we-can-make-it-manageable.
5. Brad Smith, "As we work to protect public health, we also need to protect the income of hourly workers who support our campus," Microsoft on the Issues, 5 Mar. 2020, blogs.microsoft.com/on-the-issues/2020/03/05/covid-19-microsoft-hourly-workers/.
6. Klick Health, "COVID-19 portal," covid19.klick.com/.
7. Jessie Char, "Here's what's going on with conference organizers right now" [thread], Twitter, 5 Mar. 2020, https://twitter.com/jessiechar/status/1235685514667126786.

2 WHAT DO I TELL MY TEAM?

1. Steve Blank, "The virus survival strategy for your startup," LinkedIn Pulse, 17 Mar. 2020, www.linkedin.com/pulse/virus-survival-strategy-your-startup-steve-blank/.
2. Anne Helen Petersen, "Grieving our lives as they once were," *Culture Study*, 22 Mar. 2020, annehelen.substack.com/p/grieving-our-lives-as-they-once-were.

4 THE END OF THE BEGINNING

1. Arthur Chu, "I feel like elaborating on this" [thread], Twitter, 14 Apr. 2020, twitter.com/arthur_affect/status/1250222937057058818.
2. Scott Berinato, "That discomfort you're feeling is grief," *Harvard Business Review*, 23 Mar. 2020, hbr.org/2020/03/that-discomfort-youre-feeling-is-grief.
3. Alex Danco, "It's going to get worse," *Alex Danco's Newsletter*, 19 Apr. 2020, danco.substack.com/p/its-going-to-get-worse.

5 THIS IS NOTHING LIKE MAT LEAVE

1. Holly Brockwell, "What I'm learning from being trapped in quarantine with my ex-fiance," *The Guardian*, 20 Apr. 2020, www.theguardian.com/us-news/2020/apr/20/what-im-learning-from-being-trapped-in-quarantine-with-my-ex-fiance.
2. Lindel Eakman, "Learnings from our community," Lindel's Leap, 2 May 2020, www.ldeakman.com/archives/2020/05/learnings-from-our-community.html.

6 BUT HOW DO I KNOW THEY'RE WORKING?

1. Dianne Buckner, "No slacking allowed: Companies keep careful eye on work-from-home productivity during COVID-19," CBC News, 14 May 2020, www.cbc.ca/news/business/working-from-home-employer-monitoring-1.5561969.
2. Adam Satariano, "How my boss monitors me while I work from home," *The New York Times*, 6 May 2020 (updated 7 May 2020), www.nytimes.com/2020/05/06/technology/employee-monitoring-work-from-home-virus.html.
3. Petersen, "What sort of sacrifice it will demand," *Culture Study*, 3 May 2020, annehelen.substack.com/p/what-sort-of-sacrifice-it-will-demand.
4. See, for example, Zeynep Tom, *The Good Jobs Strategy: How the Smartest Companies Invest in Employees to Lower Costs and Boost Profits* (Amazon Publishing, 2014).

7 IS ANYONE REALLY THINKING ABOUT WORK RIGHT NOW?

1. Ijeoma Oluo, "Welcome to the anti-racism movement—Here's what you've missed," Medium, 16 Mar. 2017, medium.com/the-establishment/welcome-to-the-anti-racism-movement-heres-what-you-ve-missed-711089cb7d34.

2. "Ways you can help," blacklivesmatters.carrd.co.
3. Pariss Athena, "Hey employers: Do Black lives matter?" Black Tech Pipeline, 1 June 2020, blacktechpipeline.substack.com/p/hey-employers-do-black-lives-matter.
4. Johnathan Nightingale, "I just…fuck. This is the CEO of @shopify…" [thread], Twitter, 1 June 2020, twitter.com/johnath/status/1267556509413670924.
5. For Ontario resources, see Centre for Addiction and Mental Health (CAMH), Crisis Resources, camh.ca/en/health-info/crisis-resources.

8 ARE WE GONNA TALK ABOUT THAT ASTERISK?

1. Karyn Kwaronite, "Five findings on the importance of belonging," 11 May 2019, EY, ey.com/en_us/diversity-inclusiveness/ey-belonging-barometer-workplace-study.

9 YOU'D KNOW THE ANSWER FOR SIDEWALK CHALK

1. Gwen Aviles, "Landlords are targeting vulnerable tenants to solicit sex in exchange for rent, advocates say," NBC News, 17 Apr. 2020, nbcnews.com/news/us-news/landlords-are-targeting-vulnerable-tenants-solicit-sex-exchange-rent-advocates-n1186416.

10 CHECKMATE IN FIVE MOVES

1. Sean Kleefeld, "On Strips: Billy's line," Kleefeld on Comics, 27 Feb. 2015, kleefeldoncomics.com/2015/02/on-strips-billys-line.html.
2. Emily Flitter, "'I can't keep doing this': Small-business owners are giving up," *The New York Times*, 13 July 2020, nytimes.com/2020/07/13/business/small-businesses-coronavirus.html.
3. Brooklyn Neustaeter, "Canada expected to see spike in divorces as courts reopen, lawyers say," CTV News, 18 June 2020, ctvnews.ca/health/coronavirus/canada-expected-to-see-spike-in-divorces-as-courts-reopen-lawyers-say-1.4989965.

11 THE WAITING IS THE HARDEST PART

1. See Chapter 4, "The End of the Beginning."
2. See Chapter 3, "Top 10%, Bottom 10%."
3. Jason Hehir, dir., *The Last Dance* [miniseries], Netflix, 2020.
4. Lana Wilson, dir., feat. Taylor Swift, *Miss Americana* [documentary], Netflix, 2020.
5. Ian Bonhôte and Peter Ettedgui, dir., written by Peter Ettedgui, *McQueen* [film], 2018.

6. Jay-Z, *The Blueprint 3* [album], Roc Nation, 2009, and *4:44* [album], Roc Nation, 2017.

12 JUST BECAUSE YOU HAVE WI-FI DOESN'T MEAN YOU'RE CONNECTED

1. Jeff Green, "The pandemic workday is 48 minutes longer and has more meetings," Bloomberg Business, 3 Aug. 2020, bloomberg.com/news/articles/2020-08-03/the-pandemic-workday-is-48-minutes-longer-and-has-more-meetings.
2. Michelle F. Davis and Jeff Green, "Three hours longer, the pandemic workday has obliterated work-life balance," Bloomberg Business, 23 Apr. 2020, bloomberg.com/news/articles/2020-08-03/the-pandemic-workday-is-48-minutes-longer-and-has-more-meetings.
3. ZJ Hadley, "It's time to take a break (Yes, I mean you.)," 3 July 2020, medium.com/@zj.hadley/its-time-to-take-a-break-6cdde8160bc0.
4. See Chapter 9, "You'd Know the Answer for Sidewalk Chalk."

13 CHEERFUL SWEARING FOR A CHANGE

1. See Chapter 11, "The Waiting Is the Hardest Part."

14 262,800 MINUTES

1. Kate Murphy, "We're all socially awkward now," *The New York Times*, 1 Sept. 2020, nytimes.com/2020/09/01/sunday-review/coronavirus-socially-awkward.html.
2. See Chapter 13, "Just Because You Have Wi-Fi Doesn't Mean You're Connected."
3. Christine M. Riordan, "We all need friends at work," *Harvard Business Review*, 3 July 2013, hbr.org/2013/07/we-all-need-friends-at-work.
4. Tammy Chen, "A dentist sees more cracked teeth. What's going on?" *The New York Times*, 8 Sept. 2020, nytimes.com/2020/09/08/well/live/dentists-tooth-teeth-cracks-fractures-coronavirus-stress-grinding.html.

15 HOW TO QUIT YOUR JOB DURING A PANDEMIC

1. Atlassian, "Trade-offs," www.atlassian.com/team-playbook/plays/trade-offs.
2. See Chapter 8, "Are We Gonna Talk about That Asterisk?"

16 COMPANIES DON'T MAKE DECISIONS—PEOPLE DO

1. Ibram X. Kendi, *How to Be an Antiracist* (One World, 2019).
2. Brian Armstrong, "Coinbase is a mission focused company," The Coinbase Blog, 27 Sept. 2020, blog.coinbase.com/coinbase-is-a-mission-focused-company-af882df8804.

3. Melissa Nightingale, "Last year we got our @BCorporation certification..." [thread], Twitter, 24 Sept. 2020, twitter.com/shappy/status/1309308927046189057; Johnathan Nightingale, "Lotta folks have been asking us today about Hootsuite and ICE..." [thread], Twitter, 24 Sept. 2020, twitter.com/johnath/status/1309316471160532995.
4. Sam, "Been debating talking about this publicly..." [thread], Twitter, 23 Sept. 2020, twitter.com/samelaanderson/status/1308917007438483457.
5. Johnathan Nightingale, "What can you say about this? It's ghoulish..." [thread], Twitter, 26 Aug. 2020, twitter.com/johnath/status/1298778308528701441.
6. See Ch. 14, "How to Quit Your Job During a Pandemic."

17 IS IT OKAY IF I EAT WHILE WE TALK?

1. Zeynep Tufekci, "This overlooked variable is the key to the pandemic," *The Atlantic*, 30 Sept. 2020, theatlantic.com/health/archive/2020/09/k-overlooked-variable-driving-pandemic/616548/.
2. Kara Swisher, "The man behind America's race for a vaccine," *The New York Times*, 5 Oct. 2020, www.nytimes.com/2020/10/05/opinion/sway-kara-swisher-moncef-slaoui.html. This interview sounds more dated now, since the results of the vaccine trials are all known. But when it came out, when we were writing about it, it was the clearest any government or quasi-governmental official had been about the state of progress and, even in hindsight, it's quite impressive how much he got right. This was serious light-in-the-darkness stuff.
3. Jennifer Lynn Barnes, "One time, I was at a Q&A with Nora Roberts..." [thread], Twitter, 22 Jan. 2020, twitter.com/jenlynnbarnes/status/1220182162118451200.

18 READ THIS FIRST

1. See Chapter 2, "What Do I Tell My Team?"
2. See Chapter 16, "Companies Don't Make Decisions—People Do."

19 BUT WE'RE BEING REALLY CAREFUL

1. Mickaël Causse, Patrice Péran, Frédéric Dehais, Chiara Falletta Caravasso, Thomas Zeffiro, Umberto Sabatini, and Josette Pastor, "Affective decision making under uncertainty during a plausible aviation task: An FMRI study," *Neoroimage*, vol. 71 (2013): 19–29, doi.org/10.1016/j.neuroimage.2012.12.060; Ariane Haller and Lars Schwabe, "Sunk costs in the human brain," *Neoroimage*, vol. 97 (2014): 127–33, doi.org/10.1016/j.neuroimage.2014.04.036; Jerry Suls, Jason P. Rose, Paul D. Windschitl, and Andrew R. Smith,

"Optimism following a tornado disaster," *Personality and Social Psychology Bulletin*, vol. 39 (2013): 691–702, doi.org/10.1177/0146167213477457.
2. Vicky Mochama, "How dare you?: Kim Kardashian's 40th birthday, an investigation," 28 Oct. 2020, vickymochama.medium.com/how-dare-you-kim-kardashians-40th-birthday-an-investigation-766dc879eb23.

20 EVIDENCE-BASED HOPE

1. Paul Bradley Carr, "Tony," 29 Nov. 2020, paulbradleycarr.com/2020/11/29/tony/; Sarah Lacy, "The heartbreaking loss of Tony," LinkedIn Pulse, 28 Nov. 2020, www.linkedin.com/pulse/heartbreaking-loss-tony-sarah-lacy/.
2. Carr, "A Holocracy of dunces," 3 July 2015, Pando, pando.com/2015/07/03/holacracy-dunces/.
3. Andy Doyle, "Management and organization at Medium," Medium, 4 Mar. 2016, blog.medium.com/management-and-organization-at-medium-2228cc9d93e9; Leo Widrich, "What we got wrong about self-management: Embracing natural hierarchy at work," Buffer, 5 Aug. 2015, buffer.com/resources/self-management-hierarchy/.
4. Simon Mont, "Autopsy of a failed Holacracy: Lessons in justice, equity, and self-management," *NPQ: Nonprofit Quarterly*, 9 Jan. 2017, nonprofitquarterly.org/autopsy-failed-holacracy-lessons-justice-equity-self-management/.
5. Aimee Groth, "Zappos has quietly backed away from holacracy," Yahoo! Finance, 29 Jan. 2020, finance.yahoo.com/news/zappos-quietly-backed-away-holacracy-090102533.html.

21 IT'S NOT REST IF YOU CAN'T SLEEP

1. Eve Peyser, "The people who actually had a pretty great year," *The New York Times*, 14 Dec. 2020, nytimes.com/2020/12/14/opinion/sunday/the-people-who-actually-had-a-pretty-great-year.html.

22 HAS YOUR EYE STOPPED TWITCHING YET?

1. "Giving thanks can make you happier," *Healthbeat* (Harvard Medical School), Nov. 2011, health.harvard.edu/healthbeat/giving-thanks-can-make-you-happier.

23 WHO TELLS YOU NO?

1. See Chapter 16, "Companies Don't Make Decisions—People Do."
2. Raw Signal Group, "Small business, big stakes," 20 Feb. 2020, mailchi.mp/b8d7fd3da237/small-business-big-stakes?e=b5fcb6bcc9.

24 IF THERE'S LIGHT AT THE END OF THE TUNNEL, WHY IS IT STILL SO DARK?

1. Berinato, "That discomfort you're feeling is grief."
2. Douglas Soltys, "Black Swan #35: Pandemic Year Two Action Plan" [podcast], *The Betakit Podcast*, ep. 35, 11 Jan. 2021, betakit.com/pandemic-year-two-action-plan/.
3. Vaidehi Joshi, "i miss having the mental and emotional bandwidth..." [tweet and replies], Twitter, 24 Jan. 2021, twitter.com/vaidehijoshi/status/1353490885078523905.
4. See Chapter 3, "Top 10%, Bottom 10%"

25 HOVERING OVER DECLINE AND CLICKING ACCEPT

1. "Americans waste, throw away nearly half their food: Study," Reuters, 21 Aug. 2012, reuters.com/article/us-food-waste-idUSBRE87K0WR20120821.
2. Sheera Frenkel, "Lately, I've had a some mom friends congratulate me..." [thread], Twitter, 5 Feb. 2021, twitter.com/sheeraf/status/1357824238988578817.
3. Johnathan Nightingale and Melissa Nightingale, *How F*cked Up Is Your Management? An Uncomfortable Conversation about Modern Leadership* (Raw Signal Press, 2017).
4. Jessica Bennet, photographs by Brenda Ann Kenneally, "Three American mothers, on the brink," *The New York Times*, 4 Feb. 2021, nytimes.com/interactive/2021/02/04/parenting/covid-pandemic-mothers-primal-scream.html.
5. Lucy Meakin, "Remote working's longer hours are new normal for many," Bloomberg Wealth, 2 Feb. 2021, bloomberg.com/news/articles/2021-02-02/remote-working-s-longer-hours-are-new-normal-for-many-chart.
6. Matthew Walker, *Why We Sleep: Unlocking the Power of Sleep and Dreams* (Scribner, 2017).

26 THE BEGINNING OF THE END

1. Heather Chelan, "Idk who needs to hear this but some of y'all need to know the pandemic isn't over..." [video], TikTok, 30 July 2020, tiktok.com/@hebontheweb/video/6855294017148570885.
2. Tony Plohetski, "As mayor urged Austin to 'stay home,' he was vacationing in Mexico following daughter's wedding," KVUE, 2 Dec. 2020, kvue.com/article/news/investigations/defenders/austin-mayor-steve-adler-coronavirus-covid-19-daughter-wedding-vacation/269-d76bf9b8-54bb-4736-9b00-80fdf2953145; Canadian Press, "A list of all the Canadian politicians who vacationed abroad while you locked down," *National Post*, 3 Jan. 2021,

updated 4 Jan. 2021, nationalpost.com/news/canada/a-list-of-politicians-who-travelled-abroad-despite-pandemic-era-advice-to-stay-home.
3. Catherine Porter, "Positive coronavirus test? Canadians worry their neighbors will find out," *The New York Times*, 2 Feb. 2021, nytimes.com/2021/02/21/world/canada/coronavirus-public-shaming.html

27 CAN YOU TALK ABOUT WHY EVERYONE IS QUITTING?

1. See Chapter 5, "This Is Nothing Like Mat Leave."
2. See Chapter 8, "Are We Gonna Talk about That Asterisk?"
3. See Chapter 10, "Checkmate in Five Moves."
4. See Chapter 15, "How to Quit Your Job During a Pandemic."
5. Alison Green, "I accidentally flashed my team during a video call," Ask a Manager, 15 Apr. 2020, askamanager.org/2020/04/i-accidentally-flashed-my-team-during-a-video-call.html.
6. See Chapter 1, "Our Job Now Is to Flatten the Curve."

28 ELIJAH, YOU NEED TO UNMUTE

1. Farhad Manjoo, "Do you really need to fly?" *The New York Times*, 10 Mar. 2021, nytimes.com/2021/03/10/opinion/business-travel-videoconferencing.html.
2. Jon Markoff, "The boss is robotic, and rolling up behind you," *The New York Times*, 4 Sept. 2010, nytimes.com/2010/09/05/science/05robots.html.

EPILOGUE IT'S NOT WORTH IT

1. Crickett Wilder, "Bosses who can't find workers who want to work at minimum wage" [thread], Twitter, 17 May 2021, twitter.com/crickett-wilder/status/1394328661700997124?s=20.
2. Elahe Izadi, "Washingtonian staff goes on strike after CEO's op-ed about remote work," *Washington Post*, 7 May 2021, www.washingtonpost.com/media/2021/05/07/cathy-merrill-washingtonian-strike/.
3. Raw Signal Group, "Fundamentally, this is a story about power," mailchi.mp/efade9ffe3d5/fundamentally-this-is-a-story-about-power.
4. See Chapter 5, "This Is Nothing Like Mat Leave."
5. Calvin & Habs, reply to @nesto20 When Germans Find Out about Tipping in the U.S. [video], TikTok, www.tiktok.com/@calvinandhabs/video/6961117361260858630.
6. devon, "It's so exhausting being a woman in tech" [thread and replies], Twitter, 12 May 2021, twitter.com/devonbl/status/1392483508568788994.
7. "Missing stair," Geek Feminism Wiki, n.d., geekfeminism.wikia.org/wiki/Missing_stair.

Gratitude

This book was written during an impossible year, and there were so many people who helped make it possible.

First—and this really has to be first—thank you to Adrian. There isn't a way to write down the bigness of our gratitude for you. You make the impossible possible every day. You help us show up a zillion times more professional and polished than we would left to our own devices. You put up with our twin-speak and wade through the loopiness when we've been in the tank far too long. This book, and this work, would not have happened without you. ♥

Thank you to Stephanie Fysh, our editor twice over, and to Ingrid Paulson, our book designer twice over. We couldn't imagine doing this project without you both and are thrilled you agreed to come along again. Thanks also to Zoe Grams, who helped us figure out how to tell the world about this book without getting sick of our own voices. We know we are not like your other writers. Thank you all for getting us.

Thank you to every single person who read, replied to, and shared the newsletter this year. Many of you were with us the whole way along on this journey. You were patient as we experimented with a new format, kind as we figured out how to write jointly, and generous in forwarding our words to your colleagues, pasting us in Slacks, and letting us know when we wrote something that connected for you. Thank you for trusting us with your inboxes every two weeks.

And a massive thank-you to the people who helped keep our business going during the pandemic. To Tia, catching every pivot and new project with grace and making us look good. To Galen, who jumped when we had video work that needed to go fast. To Mom and Pop and their family, who kept us fed even as the pandemic kicked their own business in the shins. To our clients who didn't miss a beat as we switched from fully in-person to fully remote programming. And to our wonderful alums who are out there running shit and making us proud. We feel incredibly fortunate to do this work. Thank you for everything.

Finally, love to our family. As we write this, it's been more than a year since we've hugged any of you. We hope it won't be much longer. We can't wait.

About the Authors

Johnathan and Melissa Nightingale spend a lot of time together. This is the second book they've co-authored. In 2017, they released their first book, the overnight bestselling *How F*cked Up Is Your Management? An Uncomfortable Conversation About Modern Leadership.*

The pair also co-founded Raw Signal Group where they provide the best management training on the planet for fast-growing orgs. Johnathan and Melissa have worked with thousands of leaders across the globe. They also write a wildly popular biweekly newsletter on management and leadership topics.

Prior to Raw Signal Group, the Nightingales worked in tech for 20 years. Between them, they've run every part of a start-up and learned a lot along the way about how to grow teams. They met in the early days of Mozilla and have been collaborating in one form or another ever since.

Johnathan and Melissa both live in Toronto, in the same house, and they still haven't run out of things to talk about.